the miniverse

the miniverse

discover an astonishing world under the microscope

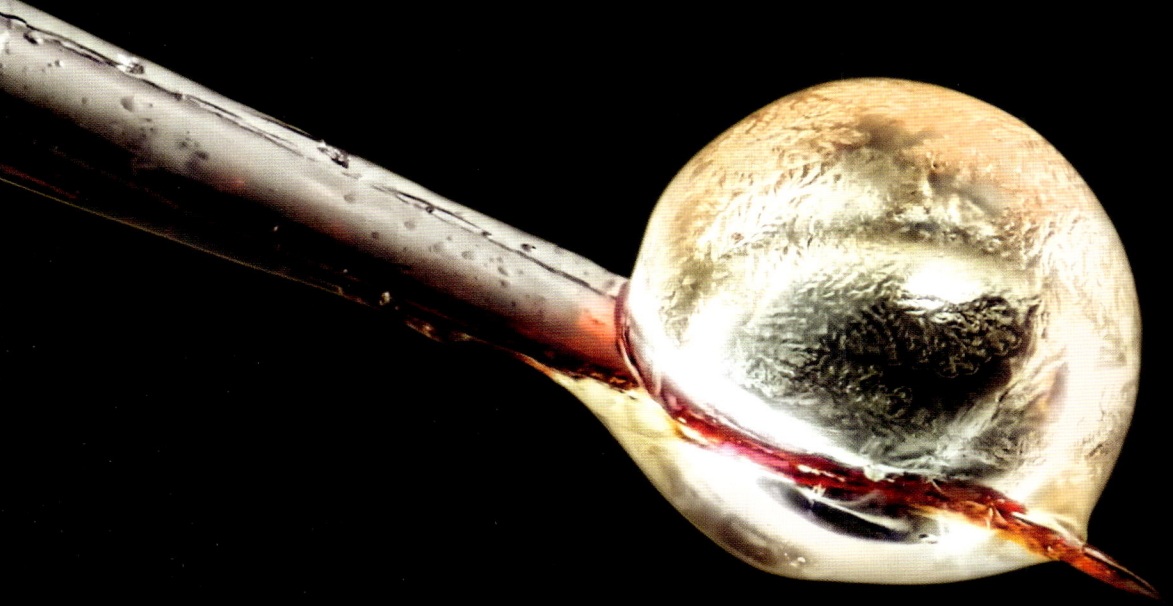

Contents

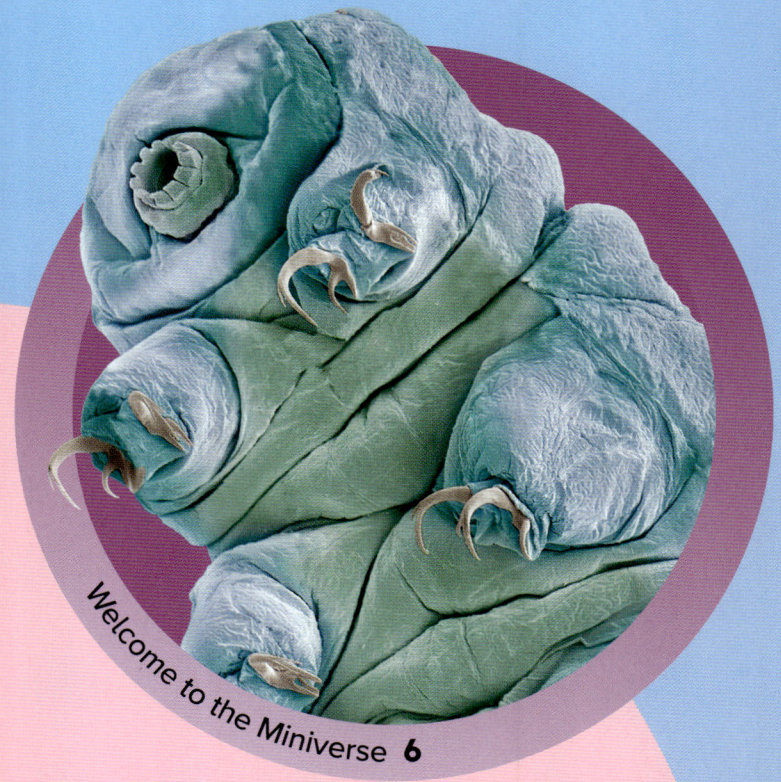

Welcome to the Miniverse 6

Velcro	12	Carrier bag	42
Zip	14	Polystyrene cup	44
Ballpoint pen	16	Razor blade	46
Felt-tip pen	18	Guitar string	48
Paper	20	Matchstick	50
Sticky note	22	Concrete	52
Dust	24	Rust	54
Dust mite	26		
House guests	28		
Salt	30		
Peppercorn	32		
Mould	34		
Kitchen sponge	36		
Fabric	38		
Face mask	40		

In the home

The human body

Blood	**58**
Skin	**60**
Sweat pore	**62**
Nose	**64**
Iris	**66**
Hair	**68**
Head lice	**70**
Teeth	**72**
Tongue	**74**
Body bacteria	**76**

The natural world

Water	**80**	Tardigrade	**114**
Snowflake	**82**	Tadpole	**116**
Sand	**84**	Earthworm	**118**
Chalk	**86**	Snail tongue	**120**
Bacteria	**88**	Mosquito	**122**
Algae	**90**	Spider silk	**124**
Leaf	**92**	Hornet sting	**126**
Leaf surface	**94**	Compound eye	**128**
Stinging nettle	**96**	Butterfly scale	**130**
Pollen	**98**	Peacock feather	**132**
Seed	**100**	Dragonfly wing	**134**
Daisy	**102**	Gecko foot	**136**
Strawberry	**104**	Shark skin	**138**
Banana	**106**		
Venus flytrap	**108**	Glossary	**140**
Tree rings	**110**	Index	**142**
Plankton	**112**	Acknowledgements	**144**

Welcome to the miniverse

When people invented microscopes about 400 years ago, they were amazed to discover a hidden universe of teeny tiny things the naked human eye cannot see, from the cells that make up our bodies to the zoo of tiny animals that live in dirty water. Today, microscopes can zoom in even further, magnifying things millions of times until we can see objects as tiny as atoms.

Magnification

If a microscope image shows an object at ten times its actual size, we say the image has 10x magnification. A good light microscope goes up to 1,000x magnification. To go beyond that you need to use an electron microscope.

Light microscope

The eyepiece magnifies 10 times.

Objective lenses magnify 10–100 times.

Glass slide holding microscopic object

Light source

Cells

The light microscope uses glass lenses to focus light and magnify images a few hundred times. In most light microscopes, the light passes through the object, so the object must be either very thin or so tiny it can float in a drop of water. Light microscopes are very good for viewing living cells.

Actual size

x5 magnification

x100 magnification

Scanning electron microscope

Peacock feather

Tapeworm

Electron microscopes use electrons (tiny particles) instead of light to create images, allowing much greater magnification. A scanning electron microscope shines a beam of electrons onto an object and makes images with the electrons that bounce off. This produces beautiful 3D pictures with light and shade. They are black and white, but colour may be added artificially.

Macro camera

Professional cameras and even some phones have special lenses to photograph tiny objects. The pictures are called macrophotographs and can reveal incredible details on insects and other small animals. It's difficult to get everything in focus in a macrophotograph. Professional photographers get round this by taking lots of pictures and using software to combine them.

Electron microscopes can **magnify** up to **10 million** times.

Transmission electron microscope

The black spots are silicon atoms.

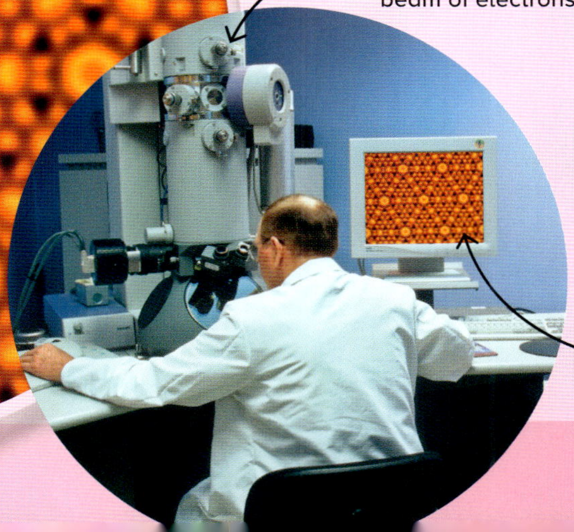

A tall, airless tube is used to generate the beam of electrons.

Image captured on screen

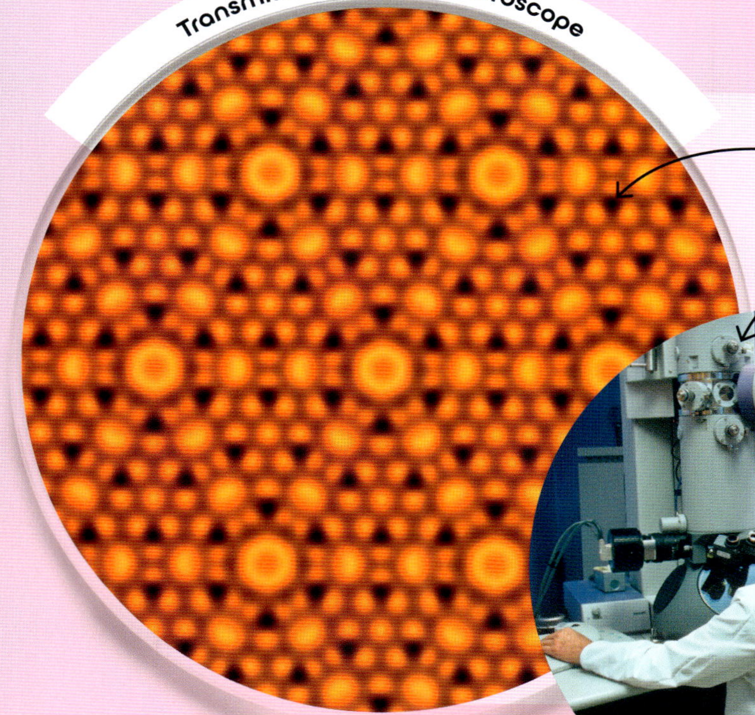

A transmission electron microscope shines a beam of electrons through objects, giving phenomenal magnification. The image here shows silicon atoms magnified 8 million times. Scientists use transmission electron microscopes to study the tiny structures that are found inside living cells.

The scale of tiny things

Tiny objects need tiny units. We measure the size of microorganisms in units called micrometres (μm). One micrometre is a thousandth of a millimetre — human hair is 75 micrometres wide. At smaller scales we use nanometres (nm). One nanometre is a millionth of a millimetre, which is about the size of a sugar molecule.

Bacteria are so tiny that 3,000 could fit on the point of a sewing needle.

100 nm (0.1 μm)
Influenza virus
This is the germ that gives people flu.

2 μm
Bacterium
Bacteria are the smallest single-celled organisms. They live everywhere, including all over you and inside you.

7 μm
Red blood cell
One teaspoon of your blood contains 25 billion red blood cells. They carry oxygen around your body.

90 μm
Pollen
Pollen grains are made in flowers and stick to bees and other pollinating insects, which help flowers reproduce.

300 μm
Dust mite
These tiny animals are related to spiders but are too small to see. They live in our homes and feed on the dead skin flakes that fall off us.

Flu virus — Bacterium — Red blood cell — Pollen — Dust mite

← Smaller

0.5–1 mm
Salt crystals are visible to the naked eye, but you need very sharp eyes to see that they have a cubic shape.

500 µm
Water bear
Also called moss piglets, water bears live in damp moss and are about half a millimetre long, making them only just visible to the naked eye.

Larger

In the home

Velcro

Found on everything from shoes to spaceships, Velcro (often known as hook-and-loop fastener) is a popular alternative to fiddly buttons and zips. Velcro consists of pairs of strips: one strip is covered in hooks and the other in loops. When pressed together, the hooks and loops intertwine to provide a secure, reusable way of fastening things together.

Inspired by nature

In 1941, while out walking, Swiss engineer George de Mestral noticed tiny seeds from a burdock had become stuck to his dog. Viewing the seeds under a microscope, de Mestral found they were covered in tiny hooks, which caught onto the dog's fur as it brushed past the plant. De Mestral was inspired to create Velcro, although it took him more than ten years to perfect his invention.

Burdock seed

Solving problems

Inventors often look to nature for solutions to engineering problems. When it was designed in the 1980s, the Japanese Shinkansen train made a loud booming noise whenever it went through a tunnel due to air resistance. To fix the problem, engineers took inspiration from the narrow beak of a kingfisher, which dives into water at high speed with barely a splash. The redesigned train was more streamlined and made much less noise when it passed through tunnels.

Kingfisher

Shinkansen

Stuck in space

Since the 1960s, astronauts have used Velcro to prevent items from floating away in the microgravity of space. They attach it to cutlery, food packets, and even the bottom of chess pieces to keep them in place. Astronauts secure their gloves and boots using Velcro, and some even stick small pieces of it inside their helmets to be used as nose scratchers.

The name Velcro comes from **combining** the first few **letters** of the **French words** *velour* (**velvet**) and *crochet* (**hook**).

One side has thousands of **loops**.

One side has thousands of **hooks**.

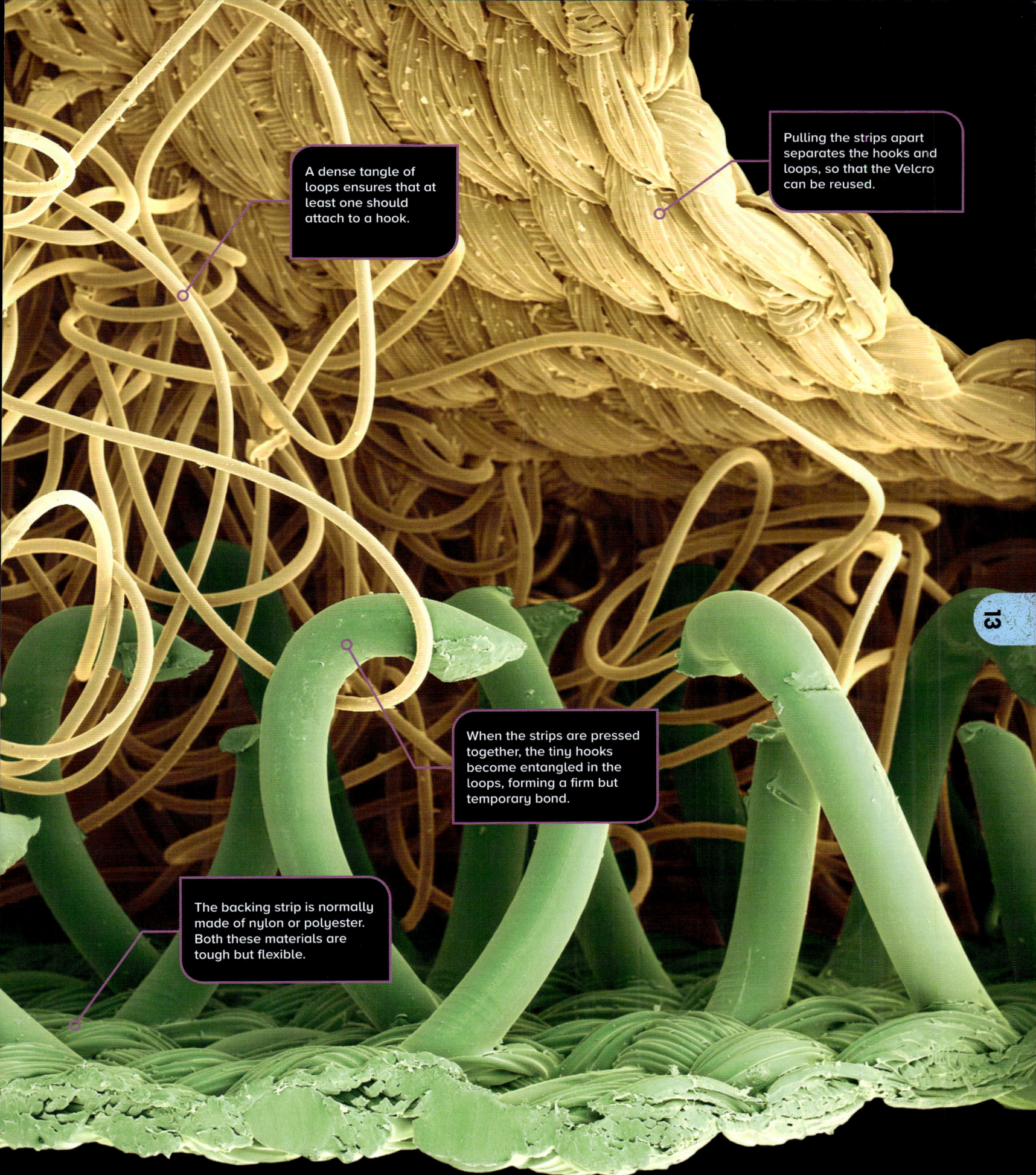

How it works: Zip

A zip does two jobs: fastening and unfastening. It does both in an instant with very little effort, which is why zips are so useful and popular.

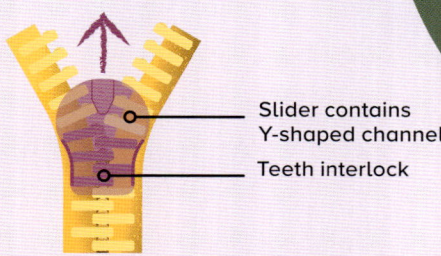

- Slider contains Y-shaped channel
- Teeth interlock

Zipping up
Pulling up the slider guides the two strips of teeth through a Y-shaped channel, forcing them to lock together.

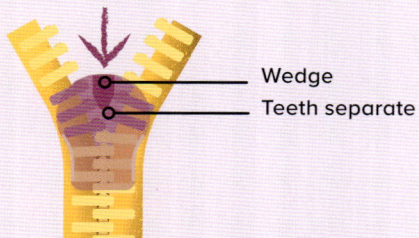

- Wedge
- Teeth separate

Unzipping
Inside the slider is a small triangular wedge. When pulled downwards, the wedge pushes the teeth sideways to separate them.

Wedges

A wedge is a type of simple machine. It is triangular in shape, narrowing to form a thin edge. One example is an axe. When you swing an axe to chop wood, the powerful downward force is converted to two outward forces that split the wood. This makes it possible to divide a log in two, which would be almost impossible with bare hands.

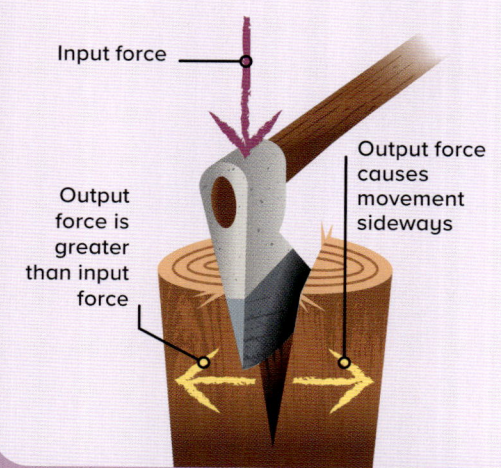

- Input force
- Output force is greater than input force
- Output force causes movement sideways

Enough zips are made in a year to wrap around Earth over 80 times.

Zip

Zips are everywhere, from pencil cases and coats to tents and even space suits. Looking closely at a zip reveals its working parts — two rows of tiny teeth, each with a hook (shaped like a bump) and a hollow (an indent). Once interlocked, these teeth are almost impossible to pull apart.

Extreme zips

The techniques and materials used to manufacture zips have become so advanced that some are now invisible, waterproof, or even airtight. Some modern zips can function in extreme environments, from diving-suit zips that can withstand the super-high pressures of the deep ocean to spacesuit zips that help to keep astronauts safe in space.

Flexible fabric strips, called the tape, anchor the teeth.

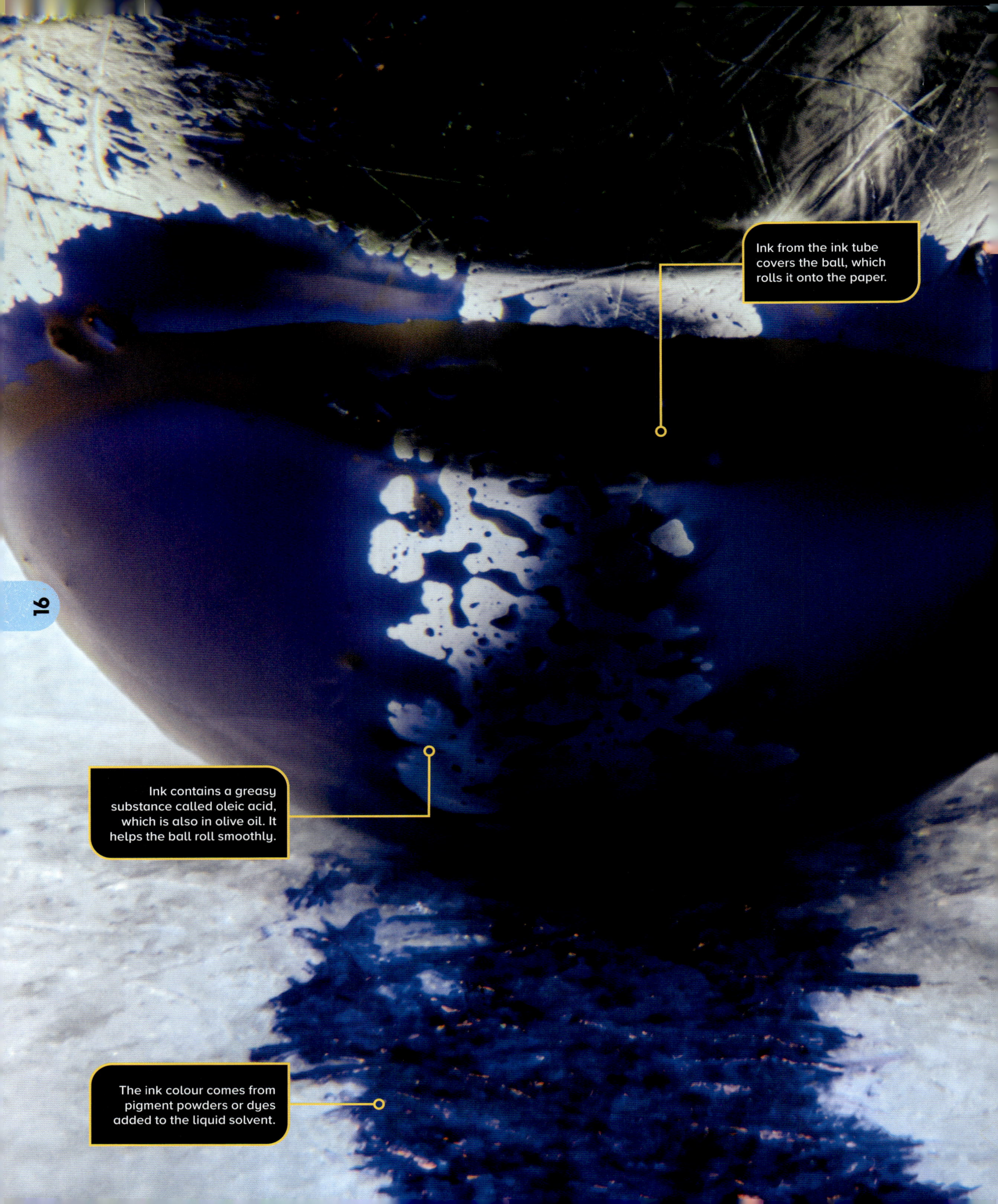

Ink from the ink tube covers the ball, which rolls it onto the paper.

Ink contains a greasy substance called oleic acid, which is also in olive oil. It helps the ball roll smoothly.

The ink colour comes from pigment powders or dyes added to the liquid solvent.

Ballpoint pen

Frustrated with messy fountain pens that leaked ink over his hands, Hungarian journalist László Bíró invented the first successful ballpoint pen. Its clever but simple design, with a tiny, rotating ball at its tip to dispense ink, is easy to use and mess-free. Today, ballpoint pens are the most popular writing instrument in the world.

How it works: Ballpoint pen

As you drag the nib of the pen across paper, friction makes the ball rotate. It picks up ink at the back and smears it onto the paper. The ball is such a precise fit that it acts like a valve, sealing the tip off from air and preventing the ink from drying out, but allowing ink to flow when it spins.

The **ink tube** contains the supply of ink, which covers the back of the ball.

The **ball** rotates to transfer ink from the ink tube to the paper.

The ball is exactly the right size to fit snugly in the tip of the pen.

The tip of a pen is called a nib.

Tiny ball

The tiny ball of a ballpoint pen is made from steel, brass, or a metal-like material called tungsten carbide that's almost as hard as diamond. The ball's smooth surface allows ink to flow continuously as it glides over paper.

What is ink made of?

Ink contains particles of pigment, which give it its colour. They are suspended in a liquid that evaporates or is absorbed when it seeps into paper, leaving the colour behind. Sticky resin acts like a glue, helping the ink to bind to the paper, ensuring any marks are permanent.

Wartime hero

During World War II, British pilots were among the first to start using ballpoint pens because they didn't leak at high altitudes the way fountain pens did.

Around **9 billion** used pens are thrown away worldwide **each year**.

Felt-tip pen

The first modern felt-tip pen was designed in Japan in 1962. It had a cartridge (container) full of ink and a soft, spongy tip made of bamboo that made a bold mark when pressed onto paper. Today, the tips of felt-tip pens are made of plastic fibres, shown here in this highly magnified image.

Invisible ink

Ultraviolet (UV) pens write with an ink that's invisible to human eyes when it dries. However, when a UV torch is shone over the ink, it glows and can be seen, making it perfect for sending secret messages. UV ink is often used to secretly label valuable objects such as laptops and smartphones, allowing them to be identified if they are stolen.

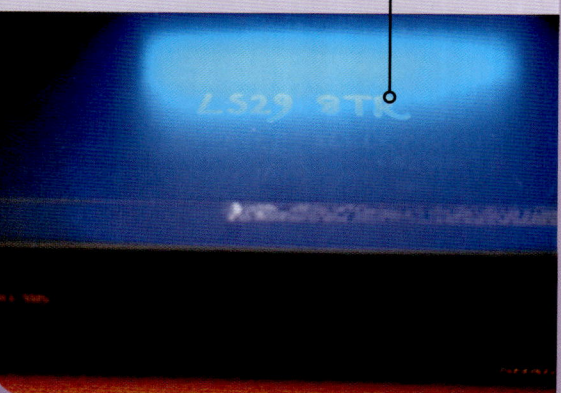

A UV torch reveals the owner's hidden code.

How it works: Felt-tip pen

Inside most felt-tip pens is a spongy core made of tightly packed fibres soaked in ink. This ink reaches the pen's tip because of a process called capillary action. This is the tendency of liquids to seep through narrow spaces because of forces of attraction between the liquid molecules and solid surfaces. As ink flows off the tip, the force of attraction pulls more ink from the reservoir, keeping the tip moist until the ink runs out.

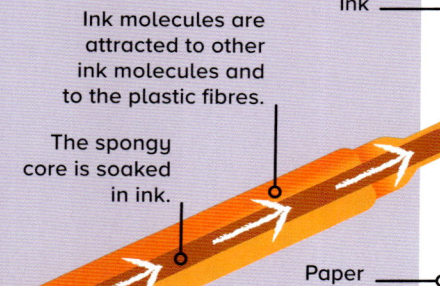

Ink molecules are attracted to other ink molecules and to the plastic fibres.

The spongy core is soaked in ink.

Ink

Paper

Dye detective

Some felt-tip inks, like green or black, are made of a mixture of colour pigments. A simple technique called chromatography can be used to identify the pigments. A spot of ink is put on a strip of absorbent paper, and one end of the paper is dipped in water. As water seeps up the paper, it carries each pigment a different distance, separating the colours in the mixture.

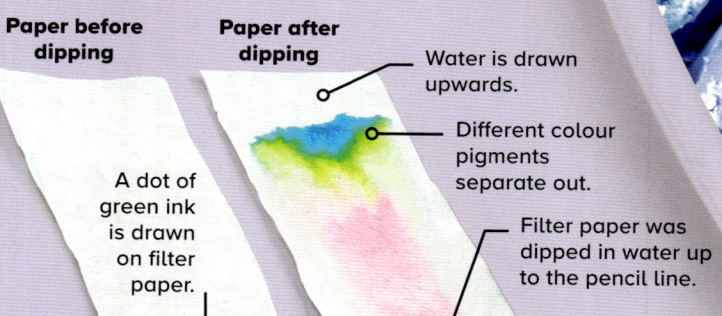

Paper before dipping

A dot of green ink is drawn on filter paper.

Paper after dipping

Water is drawn upwards.

Different colour pigments separate out.

Filter paper was dipped in water up to the pencil line.

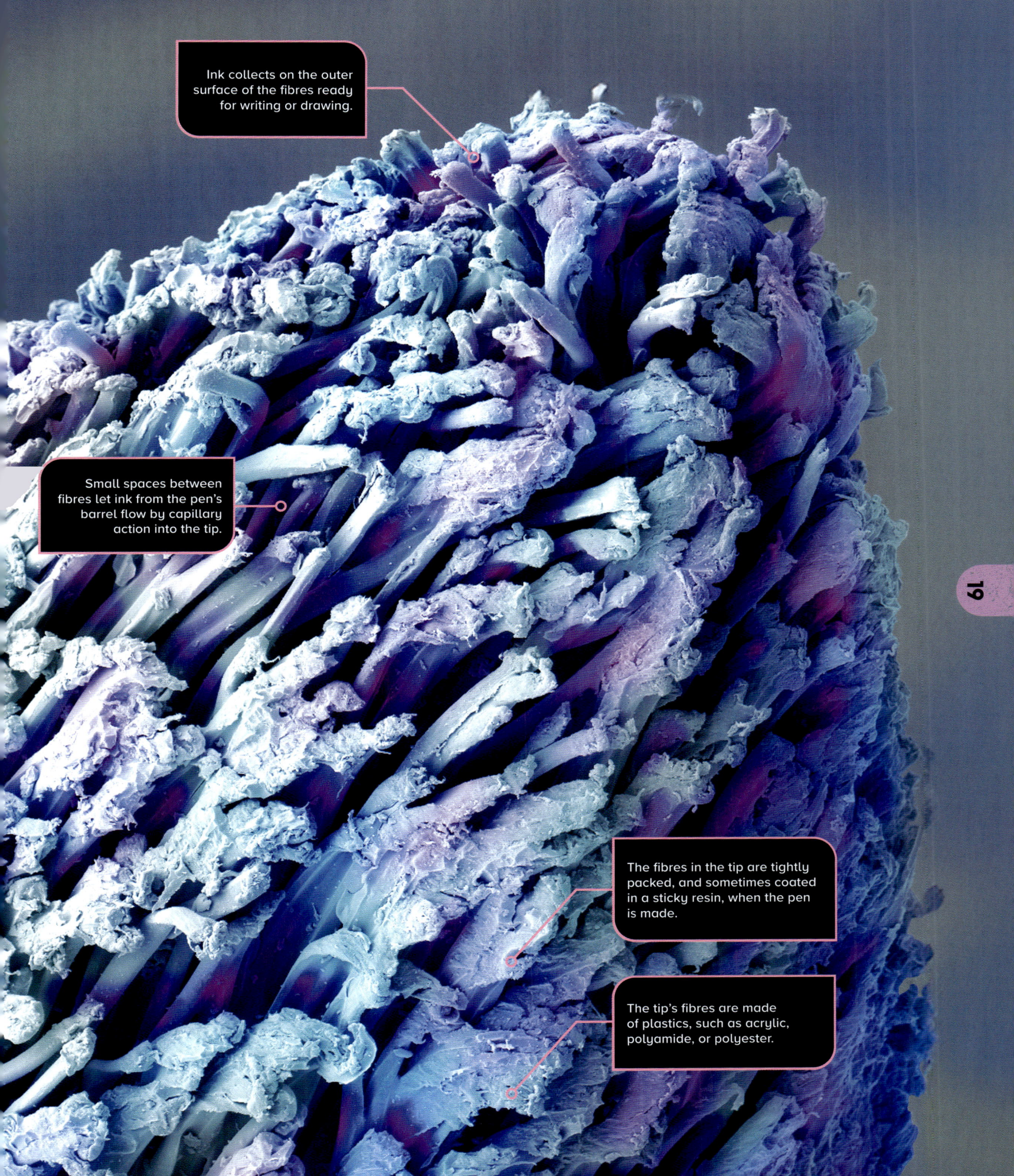

How it works: Paper

Paper is made from tiny fibres containing a material called cellulose (found in plant cell walls). These fibres can come from the wood of freshly cut trees, or recycled materials including old paper and fabrics such as cotton.

The raw material is cut and ground to separate the fibres.

Water is added to make a gloopy mixture called pulp.

Bleach, clay, chalk, or dyes may be added to change the paper's properties, depending on its intended use.

The pulp is pushed through a series of rollers to form flat sheets and remove any excess water.

The paper is ready for distribution.

Paper

Looking at paper under a microscope reveals the millions of tiny plant fibres it is made from. When torn and even when cut neatly with scissors, these thin fibres give the paper a jagged edge. Paper cuts hurt because the jagged edge acts like a saw, tearing through the skin rather than cutting it cleanly.

Why should we recycle?

Recycling waste paper uses less energy and resources than making paper from freshly cut trees. Recycling one tonne of paper saves 17 trees from being cut down, 30,000 litres of water (enough for 300 baths), and 4,000 kilowatt-hours of energy (enough to power a 5-bedroom house for a year).

Each year about **4 billion trees** are **cut down** to make paper.

Paper from poo

Many natural fibrous materials can be turned into paper. Elephant poo contains lots of undigested plant fibre that can be collected to make paper. Elephants produce up to 150 kg (330 lb) of poo a day, enough to make about 375 sheets of A4 paper.

Paper pioneer

Paper was invented in China around 105 CE by Cai Lun, a court official for the Han Emperor He. Cai Lun boiled silk rags, mulberry tree bark, bamboo, and old fishing nets, then beat them into a pulp, which he spread over a mat. The excess water drained away and the pulp dried, forming a sheet of paper. Paper wasn't made outside China for another 500 years.

When paper is torn, the fibres are pulled apart.

The fibres have been pressed into an interlocking mesh giving the paper structure.

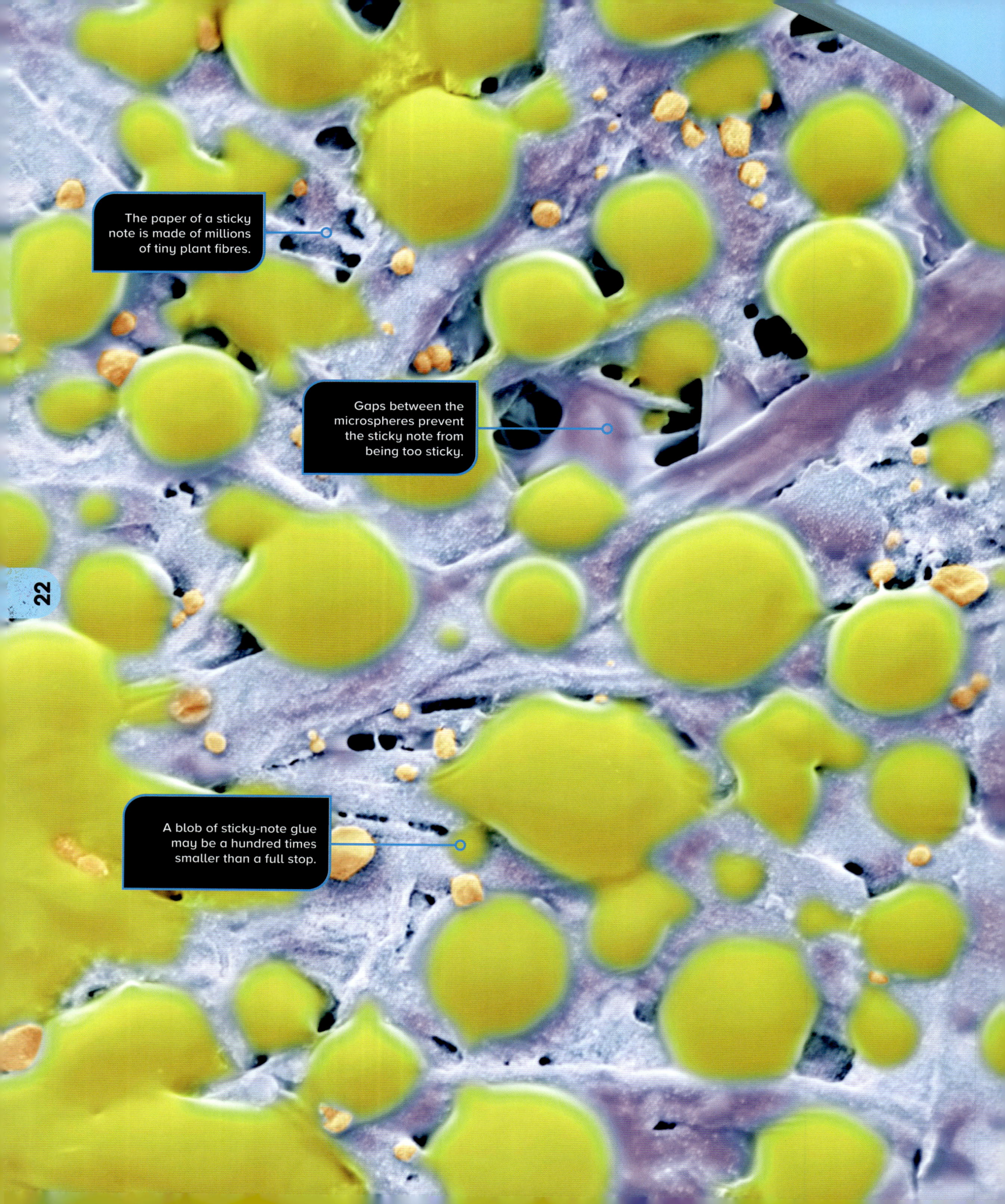

Sticky note

Some glues are super adhesive (sticky), like those able to bond stone, metal, or glass together. Others are weakly adhesive, like the glue on sticky notes, which can be easily peeled and restuck. Placed under a scanning electron microscope, the tiny blobs of glue that give sticky notes their stickiness are visible.

How it works: Sticky note

On the back of each sticky note is a strip of glue, formed of billions of tiny round blobs. When pressed onto a smooth surface, the blobs, called microspheres, are squashed and flatten out, expanding the sticky surface area of the glue in contact with its target. The glue sticks only weakly and the note can be easily repositioned or removed. When peeled, the microspheres return to their round shape to be used again.

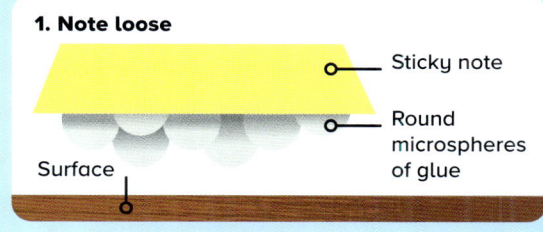

1. Note loose — Sticky note, Round microspheres of glue, Surface

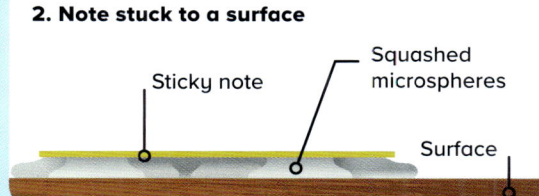

2. Note stuck to a surface — Sticky note, Squashed microspheres, Surface

There is a strip of glue on the back of the sticky note.

Shear and peel

Glues are tested for their "stickability" in different ways. Two of the tests look at shear and peel strength. Shear strength testing involves pulling in parallel but opposite directions. Peel strength testing involves pulling the two bonded surfaces apart at right angles.

Shear strength

Peel strength

Oldest glue

The oldest-known glue has been used for at least 50,000 years. Prehistoric people found that heating birch-tree bark released a sticky tar. The tar could then be used to glue stone arrowheads to wooden shafts.

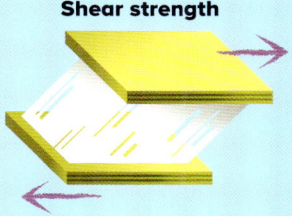
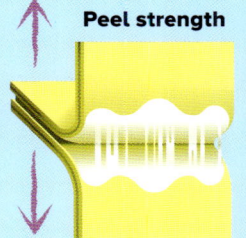

This flint arrowhead has been carved to a sharp point.

The birch tar hardens to bond the arrowhead to the shaft.

What's in dust?

Dust is an assortment of hundreds of different kinds of debris, and every home has a unique "dust fingerprint". Up to half of household dust is dead skin.

Dead skin cells

Pollen grains

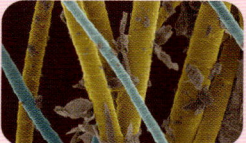
Hair

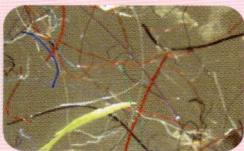
Microfibres

Sand

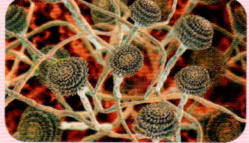
Fungal spores

The average person **sheds** more than **5 billion skin** cells **per day.**

Dust bunnies are fluffy tangles of hair, fibres, and household dust.

Plastic dust

Modern clothes, carpets, bedding, and furniture are often made of plastics such as polyester. Over time, these synthetic fabrics break up into tiny fragments called "microplastics". They pollute the air in our homes, and we breathe them in all the time. Small children breathe in the most as they play on the floor, where dust builds up.

Dust

To the naked eye, household dust is just an annoying grey powder that gets everywhere. Seen through a microscope, however, it becomes a wonderland of microscopic oddities that tell the story of our daily lives.

Cotton fibres fall off your clothes and bedding all the time.

Space dust

A small fraction of household dust comes from space. Micrometeorites are specks of rock or metal that come from comets and asteroids. An estimated 30,000 tonnes of space dust enters Earth's atmosphere every year.

Some micrometeorites melt when they enter Earth's atmosphere and become spherical.

First vacuum cleaner

In 1901, British inventor Cecil Booth demonstrated the first device that could remove dust by suction rather than merely sweeping it into the air. His vacuum cleaner parked outdoors while long hoses were fed through windows.

How it works: Dust mite life cycle

Dust mites go from egg to adult in under a month. An adult female lays 2–3 eggs per day. These hatch into wriggly larvae with six legs. They then transform into nymphs, and develop two more legs, before finally becoming adults. Adult males live for around a month but females can live up to three times as long.

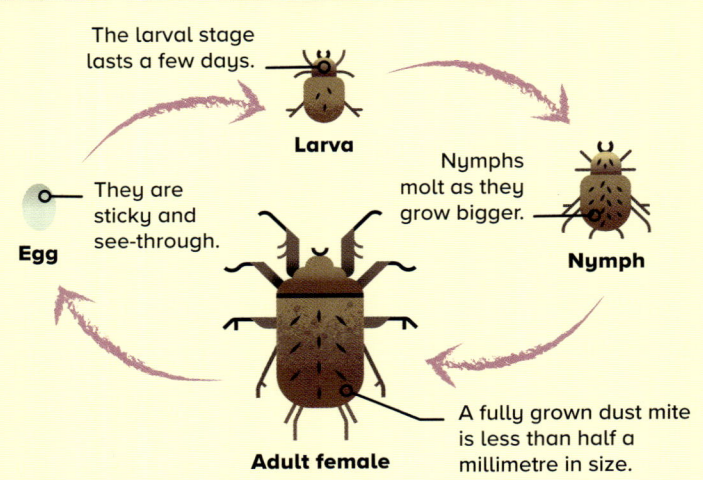

The larval stage lasts a few days.

Larva

Nymphs molt as they grow bigger.

Nymph

They are sticky and see-through.

Egg

A fully grown dust mite is less than half a millimetre in size.

Adult female

Dust mite

Creeping through the dust in your house are millions of tiny creepy-crawlies called dust mites, each about half the size of a grain of salt. They live in carpets, furniture, bedding, and every dusty surface, and they feast on the millions of dead skin cells that humans and their pets shed every single day. With no eyes, they use their keen sense of smell and touch to find food. Dust mites don't bite, but their droppings can make allergic reactions such as asthma worse.

The **average bed** contains **100,000–2,000,000** dust mites.

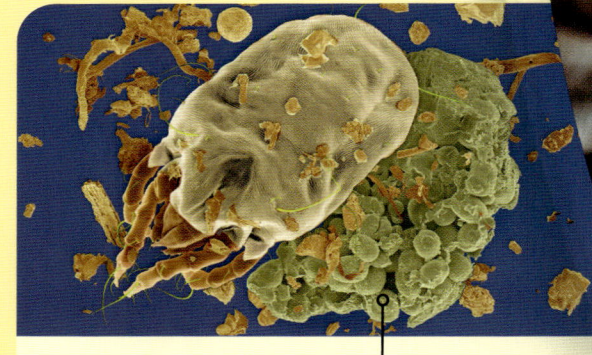

Dust mite droppings

Dust mite allergy

A dust mite poos around 200 times its own body weight during its short life. Some people are allergic to the droppings, giving them a runny or stuffy nose, a cough, and watering eyes. Sometimes, they make people's skin itchy or even cause a rash.

A bed bug uses its proboscis to pierce skin and suck blood.

Carpet beetle

Carpet beetles burrow into places like carpets, clothes, and upholstered furniture to lay their eggs. The larvae feed on natural fibres like cotton, silk, wool, and leather. Once they've settled in, they can be very hard to get rid of. They also multiply quickly — female carpet beetles can lay 100 eggs at a time.

Bed bug

Despite their name, bed bugs can live all around the house. These flat-bodied, ant-sized bugs hide in all sorts of small, dark gaps and cracks. They feed by sucking blood from mammals, including humans. Although they only suck a microscopic drop of blood each time they feed, their bites can cause rashes or allergic reactions in some people.

Fruit flies have **bright red eyes.**

Fruit fly

These sesame-seed-sized flies can be found wherever there is overripe or rotting food, from fruit bowls and rubbish bins to drains and kitchen sinks. They don't eat the rotting food itself, but the yeast that grows on it as it rots. They live fast and die young, turning from egg to larva in just 12 hours, with a typical lifespan of around a month.

A fruit fly has a specialized, spongy sucker, called a labellum, to slurp up yeast.

Cat flea

Cat fleas are parasites that mostly live on cats, but can be found on dogs and other animals too. Their flattened bodies are the perfect shape to slip between densely packed hairs as they search for the perfect spot to bite the skin and suck blood. They can consume 15 times their own body weight in blood in a day.

House guests

You might be surprised by just how many microscopic creatures live in your home. Some are big enough to spot running across walls or floors, but most are so small you never see them. They are hiding everywhere: in furniture, carpets, your bed, your clothes — even between the pages of this book.

The flat body swells to twice the size after sucking blood.

Silverfish **moult** as often as **30 times** a year.

A weevil's tiny biting jaws are at the tip of its snout.

Long antennae to smell food and find their way

The body is covered in microscopic scales.

Weevil

There are around 97,000 species of weevil. Most of these beetles eat plants, and some manage to weasel their way into kitchens and pantries. Females use their long snouts to bore into small pieces of foods, such as grains of cereals and rice, and then lay their eggs inside.

Silverfish

These silvery insects look a bit like fish as they dart about, their bodies wiggling from side to side. Silverfish love dark, damp spaces such as bathrooms and cellars. They feed on starchy materials like paper and glue, and can often be found eating books. They also eat crumbs, dead insects, and even their own moulted exoskeletons.

Salt

Sprinkle some salt on your hand and look as closely as you possibly can. You'll see that the salt grains are tiny crystal cubes, shaped like dice. Salt has this shape because its atoms build up in a simple repeating pattern. Solids that form this way are called crystals and have all sorts of geometric shapes, from cubes and cylinders to hexagons.

Ice defence

When water freezes, it forms hexagonal crystals. But if you add salt, it interferes and makes it hard for crystals to form. This has a very handy effect: it lowers the freezing point to well below 0°C (32°F). Sprinkling salt on icy roads in winter melts the ice and stops new ice forming, making driving much safer.

Salt spreader truck

Why cubes?

Salt (sodium chloride) is made of two elements: sodium and chlorine. Their atoms form particles called ions, which have opposite electric charges and so attract one another. This makes them stack in a repeating cubic pattern, each sodium surrounded by six chlorine ions and each chlorine surrounded by six sodium ions.

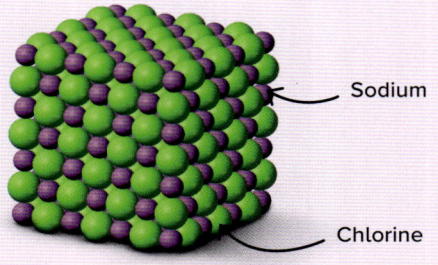

Sodium

Chlorine

Salt flats

Salt makes up about 3.5 per cent of the weight of seawater. Some deserts have "salt flats" – vast plains covered in a crust of salt left after a lake evaporated thousands of years ago. Salar de Uyuni in Bolivia is the world's largest salt flat and is as big as Jamaica. When it rains, the layer of water on the flat ground turns it into a gigantic mirror.

*Naturally occurring salt is also called **halite** or **rock salt**.*

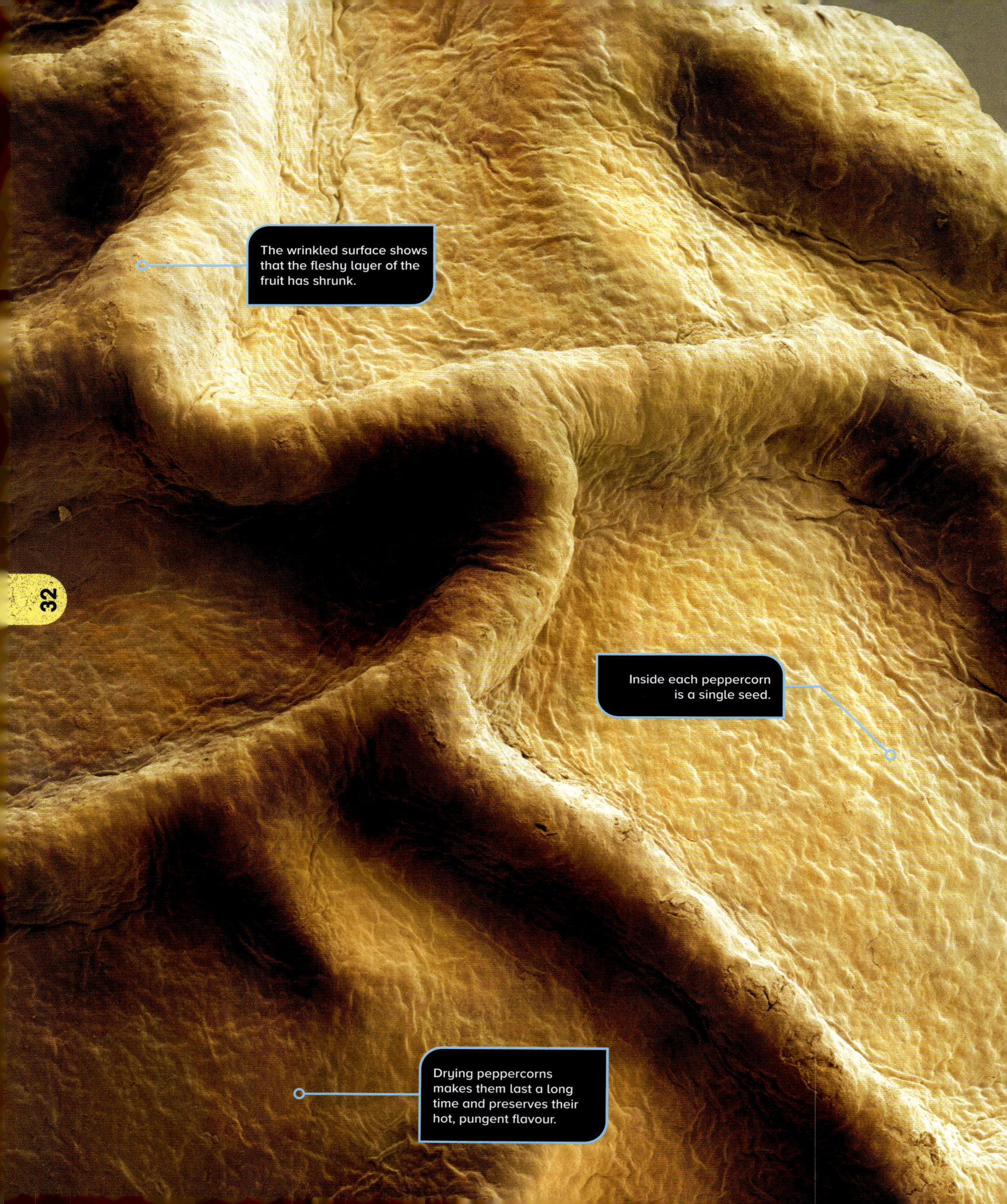

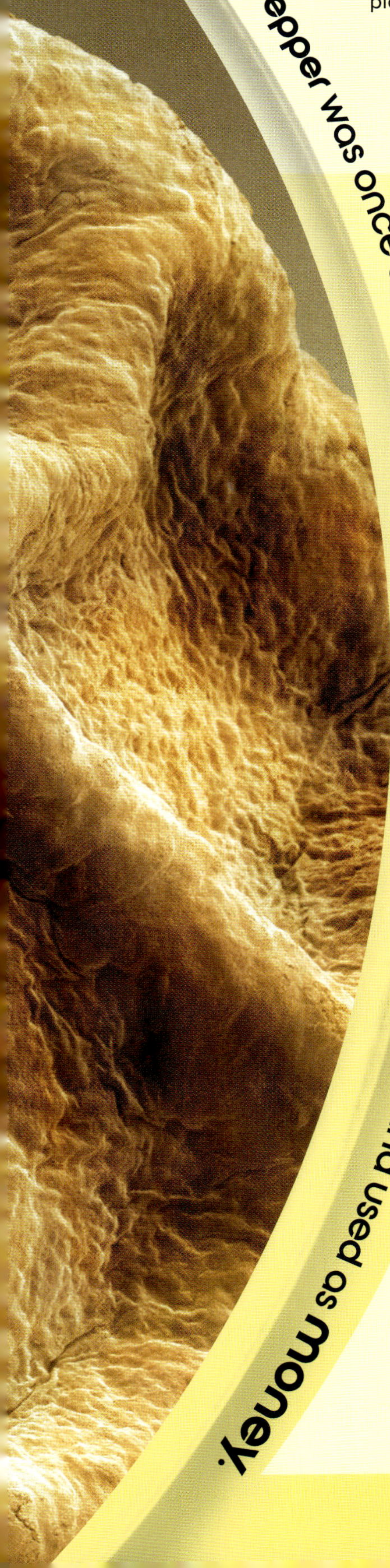

How it works: Peppercorn production

Pepper fruits are ready for harvesting about eight months after the pollination of pepper flowers. The green fruits grow in bunches called spikes. They are picked, boiled, and dried, which turns them black. The peppercorns are then threshed — separated from the stems of the spikes by hand or with a stick.

- Fresh, green pepper fruits
- Dry black peppercorns
- Fruits darken as they dry
- Boiled fruits

Peppercorn

Black pepper is the world's most common spice, adding a hot, earthy flavour to our dishes. It's made by grinding up peppercorns — the dried fruits of the black pepper vine. Roughly the size of a small hailstone, a peppercorn has a wrinkly surface, as seen here at x100 magnification.

Pepper was once so valuable that it was called black gold and used as money.

Types of peppercorn

The fruits of the black pepper plant are processed to give four different types of peppercorn.

Black peppercorns are the most common and have the strongest flavour.

White peppercorns come from pepper fruits left to turn red on the vine before harvesting. The skin is removed to reveal the smooth white seed, which is then dried. White pepper is milder in flavour.

Green peppercorns are made from green fruits picked at the same stage as black peppercorns, but they aren't allowed to dry. Instead they are pickled or freeze-dried.

Red peppercorns are the mature red fruits of the black pepper plant and are less commonly used in cooking.

Up to 80 fruits grow on each spike of a black pepper plant.

Discovery of bacteria

It may sound strange, but pepper played a key role in the discovery of bacteria. In 1676, Dutch merchant Antonie van Leeuwenhoek examined a peppercorn using a handheld microscope that he'd made. He did this to try to understand the source of pepper's spiciness. Instead, he found moving microorganisms, making him the first person to observe bacteria.

- Tiny lens to look through
- Focusing screw
- Pin to hold sample

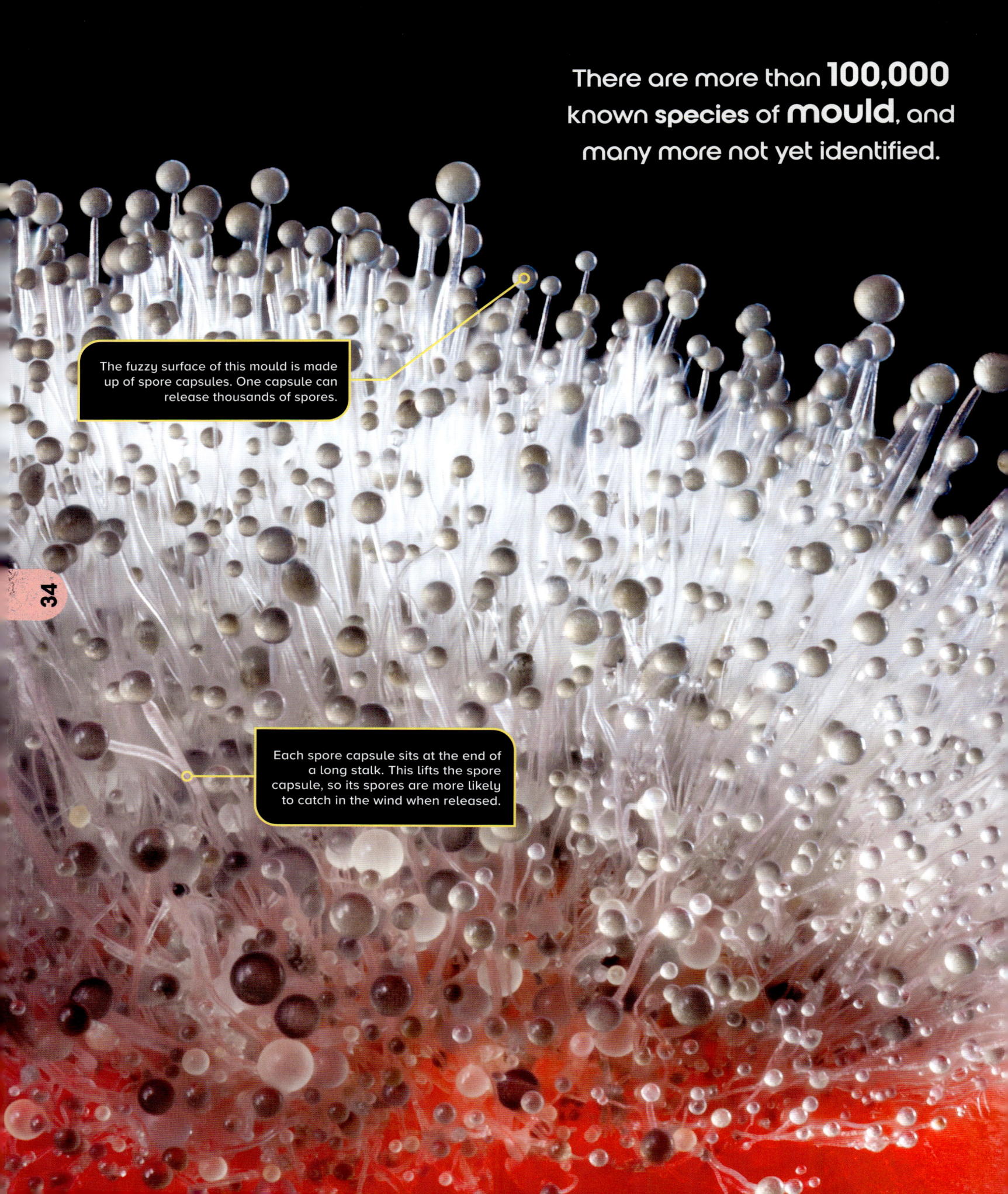

There are more than **100,000** known **species** of **mould**, and many more not yet identified.

The fuzzy surface of this mould is made up of spore capsules. One capsule can release thousands of spores.

Each spore capsule sits at the end of a long stalk. This lifts the spore capsule, so its spores are more likely to catch in the wind when released.

How it works: Mould

Mould starts as tiny airborne spores. When the spores land on the tomato, they grow into threads below its skin called hyphae, which break down and feed on the tomato's nutrients. When conditions are right, the mould grows structures that break through the tomato skin. In time, these release more spores to be scattered through the air, land elsewhere, and create new mould.

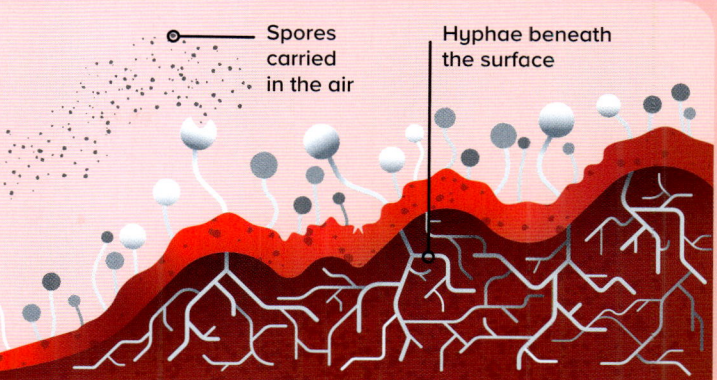

Spores carried in the air

Hyphae beneath the surface

Spore capsule

Dark spots are spore capsules

Decaying tomato

Mould

Finding blue-green mould growing on food, such as an old tomato, can be a nasty surprise. Under a microscope, however, mould becomes more intriguing. It is a type of fungus, like a mushroom, and up close you can see it is made up of tiny threads. These use nutrients in the food to grow.

Nature's recyclers

Fungi, such as these golden scalycap mushrooms, play an important role in recycling dead matter. As they feed, they release nutrients such as minerals and nitrogen into the soil. Plants absorb these nutrients and use them to grow. Without fungi, dead matter would pile up and never disappear.

Bacteria

Penicillin

In 1928, scientist Alexander Fleming noticed that a dish of bacteria he was studying had been contaminated with penicillium mould. A chemical in the mould had killed off the bacteria around it, forming a bacteria-free zone. He called this chemical penicillin, and it was later developed into the world's first antibiotic drug.

Penicillium mould

Mouldy cheese

Many cheeses have moulds intentionally added as part of the cheesemaking process. These moulds speed up the ageing process and introduce flavours and textures as they digest the cheese. Blue cheese gets its distinct flavour from the penicillium mould.

How it works: Kitchen sponge

A sponge is made up of thousands of empty spaces, all linked by a maze of narrow channels. It soaks up water because water molecules are attracted to the surface of all the holes and channels. Together, all these empty spaces have a much larger area than the sponge's outer surface. When the sponge gets wet, water fills the holes and sticks to all these inner surfaces.

Squeezing the wet sponge squashes the holes and channels, forcing out the water.

Hideout for germs

A damp kitchen sponge is the ideal home for bacteria due to its tiny holes filled with food crumbs. As many as 54 billion bacteria can live in just a pea-sized piece of a sponge — almost as many as you'll find in poo! Although most species are harmless, some bacteria can be bad for your health, so sponges need replacing regularly.

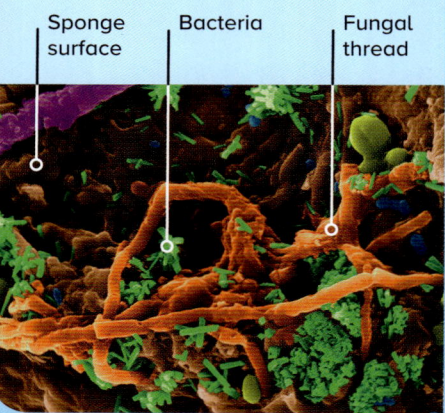

Sponge surface | Bacteria | Fungal thread

Kitchen sponge

A kitchen sponge absorbs and holds water for washing dirty dishes. Made from plastic or plant-based alternatives, sponges are soft and squishy because they are full of tiny holes. These empty spaces, and the walls separating them, increase the sponge's surface area, maximizing the amount of water it can hold.

Natural sponges

Modern plastic kitchen sponges were designed to replace natural sea sponges, which people used for thousands of years. These simple animals have no heads or mouths, and live on the seabed, rooted to the spot. Most species absorb water into their soft bodies and filter it for food and oxygen.

Dried sea sponge

Some sponges can hold more than 20 times their weight in water.

In the home — Kitchen sponge — 36

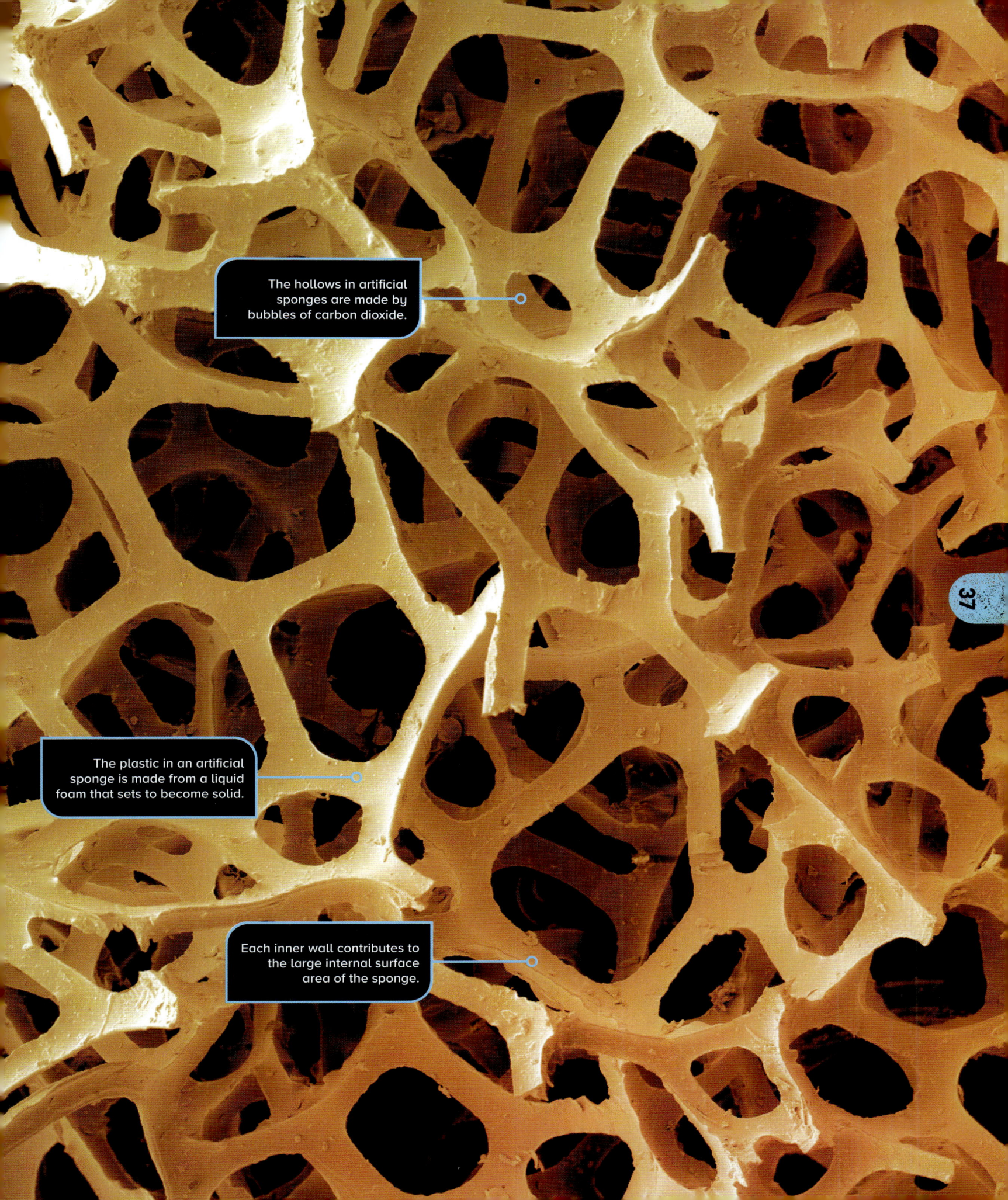

The hollows in artificial sponges are made by bubbles of carbon dioxide.

The plastic in an artificial sponge is made from a liquid foam that sets to become solid.

Each inner wall contributes to the large internal surface area of the sponge.

Silk

A symbol of luxury, silk is a shimmering, soft, and light – but very strong – natural fabric used to make wedding dresses and high-fashion items of clothing. Silk threads are made by a special kind of moth caterpillar called the mulberry silkworm as it spins a cocoon around itself. The cocoon is made of a single thread about 0.5 km (0.3 miles) long and has to be boiled to soften it for processing – which kills the caterpillar that made it.

300x magnification

Fabric

Fabrics are the flexible materials used to make things like clothes and sheets. They're made by weaving or knitting fibres together. The fibres may be natural, such as animal hair, or synthetic, made by chemical processes. Microscopes can show us how the fibres are arranged in fabrics.

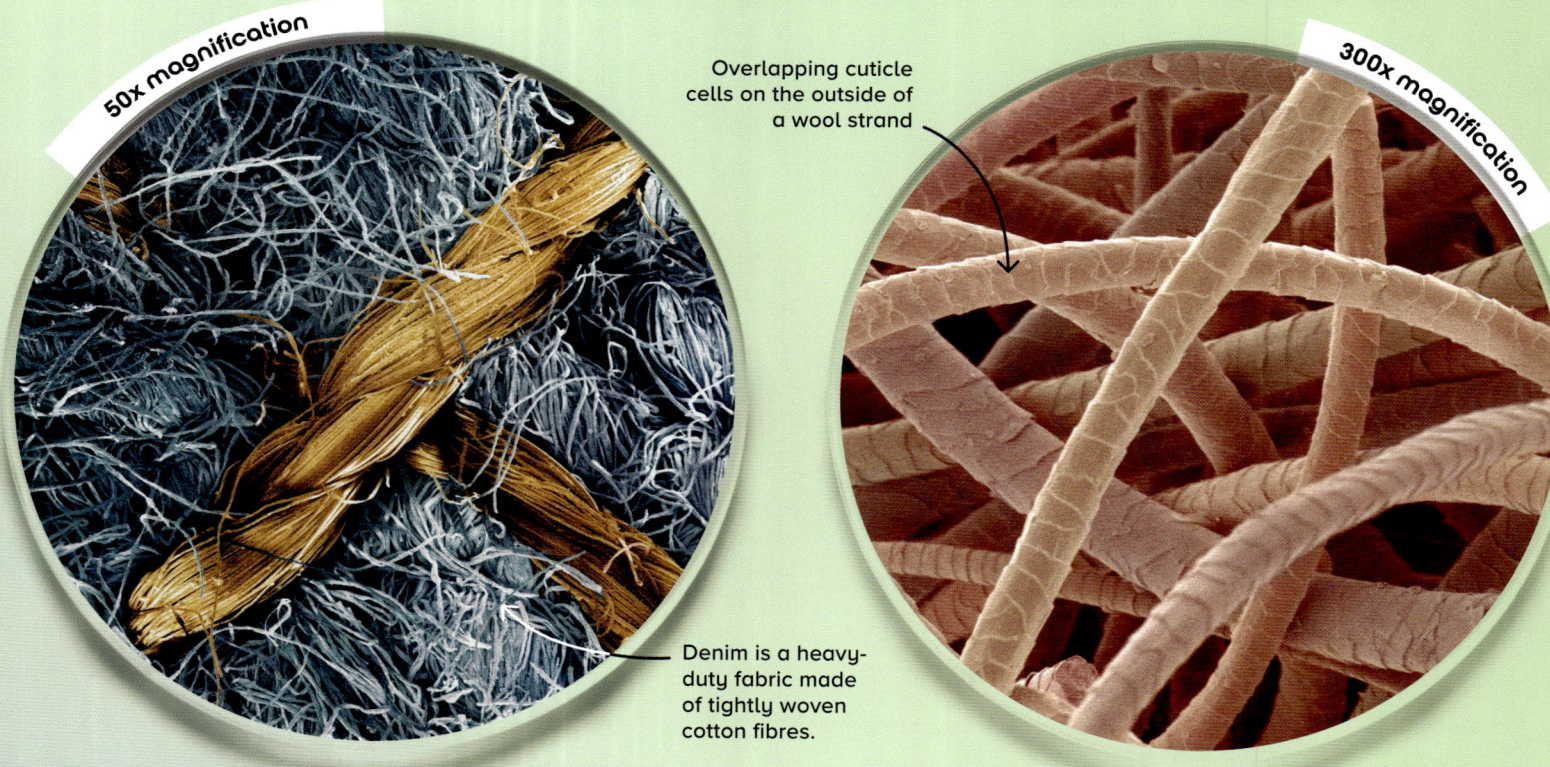

50x magnification

300x magnification

Overlapping cuticle cells on the outside of a wool strand

Denim is a heavy-duty fabric made of tightly woven cotton fibres.

Cotton

Cotton comes from the fluffy fibres produced by the seed capsules of the cotton plant. The fibres are separated from the seeds, washed, and spun into long threads. Cotton clothes are mostly soft and breathable, which means air and moisture can pass through the fabric's fibres.

Wool

Mostly produced from the coats of sheep, wool can also come from mammals such as angora goats and llamas. Strands of hair from these animals are spun together to make wool yarn (long threads), which can be knitted or woven into blankets and clothes, such as jumpers and scarves. Trapped air pockets in the fabric make it a great insulator, ideal for cold conditions.

30x magnification

50x magnification

This close-up image shows a pair of elasticated nylon tights.

Linen

Made from a plant called flax, linen is one of the oldest natural fabrics. Archaeologists have found dyed linen fibres more than 30,000 years old. For thousands of years, the ancient Egyptians used linen to wrap and preserve dead mummies. Today, it is often used to make summer clothes, because it keeps the wearer cool.

Nylon

Nylon was the first synthetic fabric. It is made of plastic fibres and was developed as a substitute for silk to make stockings, and later parachutes in World War II (1939–1945). Nylon is exceptionally strong and durable. As well as being made into clothes, it is used to make seatbelts, tents, and carpets.

Polyester

Like nylon, polyester is a plastic made from fossil fuels. Its fibres are manufactured in a range of different thicknesses, the thinnest being much finer than a silk fibre. Sports clothes, especially football shirts, are made from polyester fabrics, which are light, windproof, and resistant to wrinkles. The fabrics also wick away sweat from the body and dry quickly because the fibres do not absorb water.

40x magnification

Looser woven fibres form holes that make the fabric breathable.

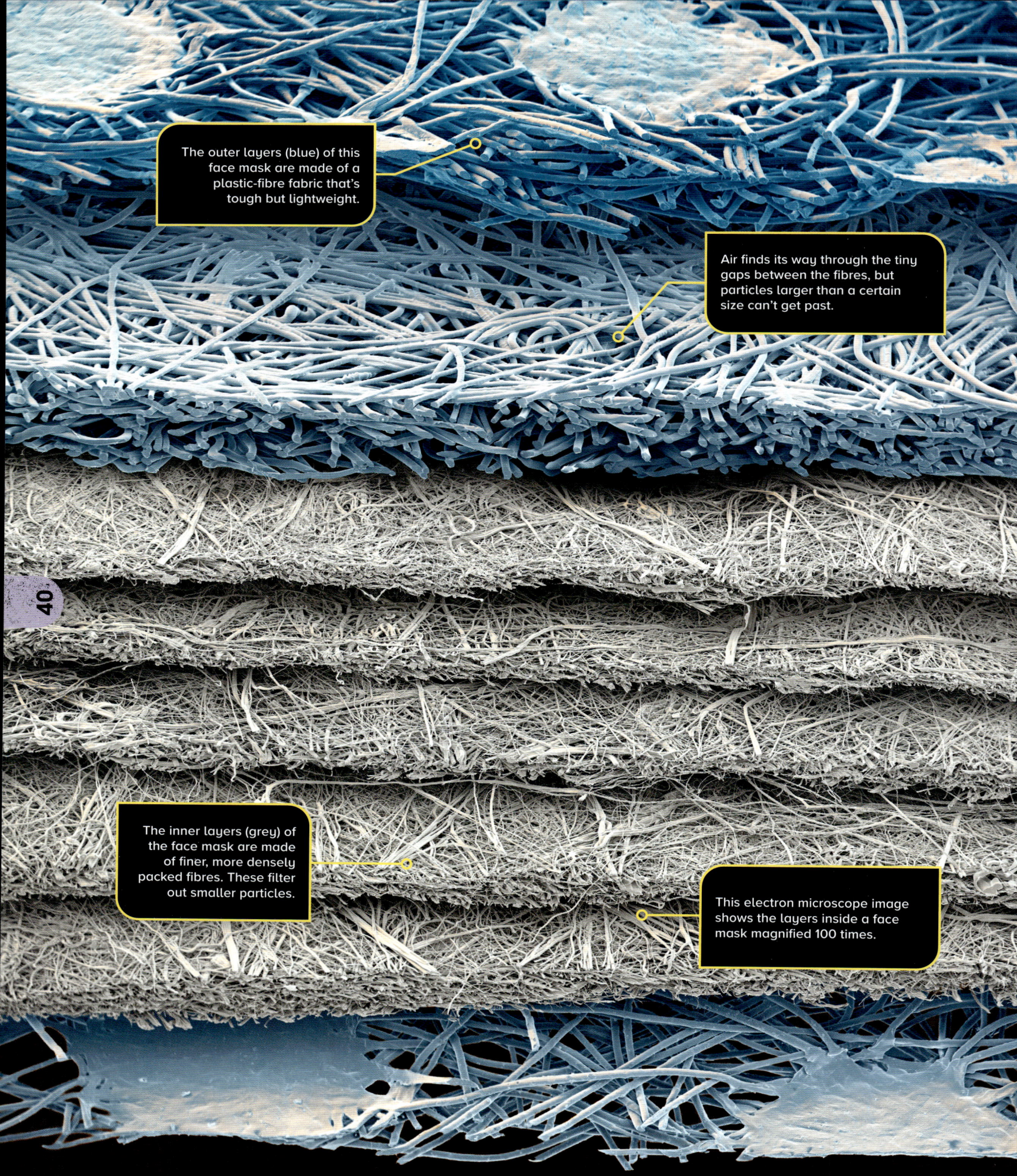

How it works: Preventing infection

Many illnesses are spread by the tiny airborne droplets in coughs, sneezes, or even speech. A face mask blocks these droplets while letting air through, which makes the wearer less likely to pass on their germs. A tightly fitting mask can also protect the wearer from inhaling other people's germs.

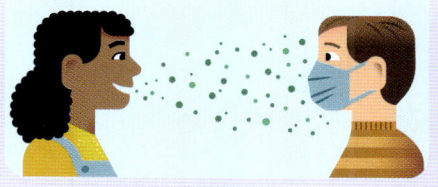
A person without a face mask releases lots of droplets into the air.

When both people wear face masks, very few droplets are released.

Face mask

The layers of tangled fibres in this face mask could save your life, or at least reduce your risk of getting ill. A face mask acts as a barrier, letting air through but trapping germs. Face masks became a common sight during the spread of the disease Covid in the early 2020s.

Layers of protection

Adding extra layers to a face mask increases the protection it provides. Each layer acts like a maze trapping any harmful particles travelling through. The more layers attached together, the more protection the mask gives.

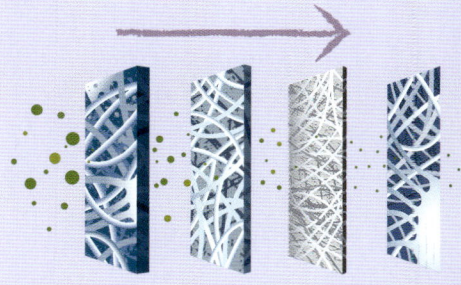

In the **first year** of the **Covid** pandemic, **379 billion** face masks were sold. That's about **50** for **every person** on the planet.

Ready for anything

A face mask doesn't always give enough protection. People with dangerous jobs, such as cleaning up chemical spills or nuclear incidents, wear full-body "hazmat" (hazardous materials) suits. The highest level of hazmat protection is an airtight suit with built-in gloves and boots. An air tank can be fitted inside to let the wearer breathe.

Both the mouth and nose should be covered when wearing a face mask.

How does plastic damage the oceans?

If plastic isn't recycled or disposed of properly, it can end up washed down drains. From there it gets washed into rivers and finally the sea. Plastic in rivers and oceans poses a huge threat to wildlife. Sea turtles, for example, often mistake carrier bags for a favourite food — jellyfish. Animals can also get trapped in plastic packaging or discarded fishing nets, causing injury, ill health, and, frequently, death.

Carrier bag

We use more than a trillion plastic bags a year. Though useful, they are bad for the environment, mainly because they stick around for a long time and break down into harmful chemicals. One solution is to switch to bags made from natural materials, like the biodegradable bag seen here, magnified 13,000 times by an electron microscope.

Biodegradable bags

Scientists have developed bags made from plants like corn, cassava, sugar cane, and sugar beet. The plant material is ground up and a substance called starch is extracted. This is then converted into a biodegradable plastic and used to make bags. The bags break down naturally after disposal, usually within a few months.

Decomposition

The process by which things break down is called decomposition. How fast something decomposes depends on what it is made from and factors such as heat and moisture. A natural material, such as a banana skin, will decompose in 2–5 weeks in the right conditions. Objects made from plastics, even recyclable ones, take far longer.

- 3–6 months — Biodegradable carrier bag
- 5 years — Juice carton
- 80 years — Crisp packet
- 450 years — Plastic bottle

This bag is as biodegradable as the food inside it.

Microplastics everywhere

As plastic breaks down, it turns into tiny fragments so light they float in the air. We breathe, eat, and drink these microplastics daily, with health impacts we are only starting to understand.

Microplastic waste in seaside sand

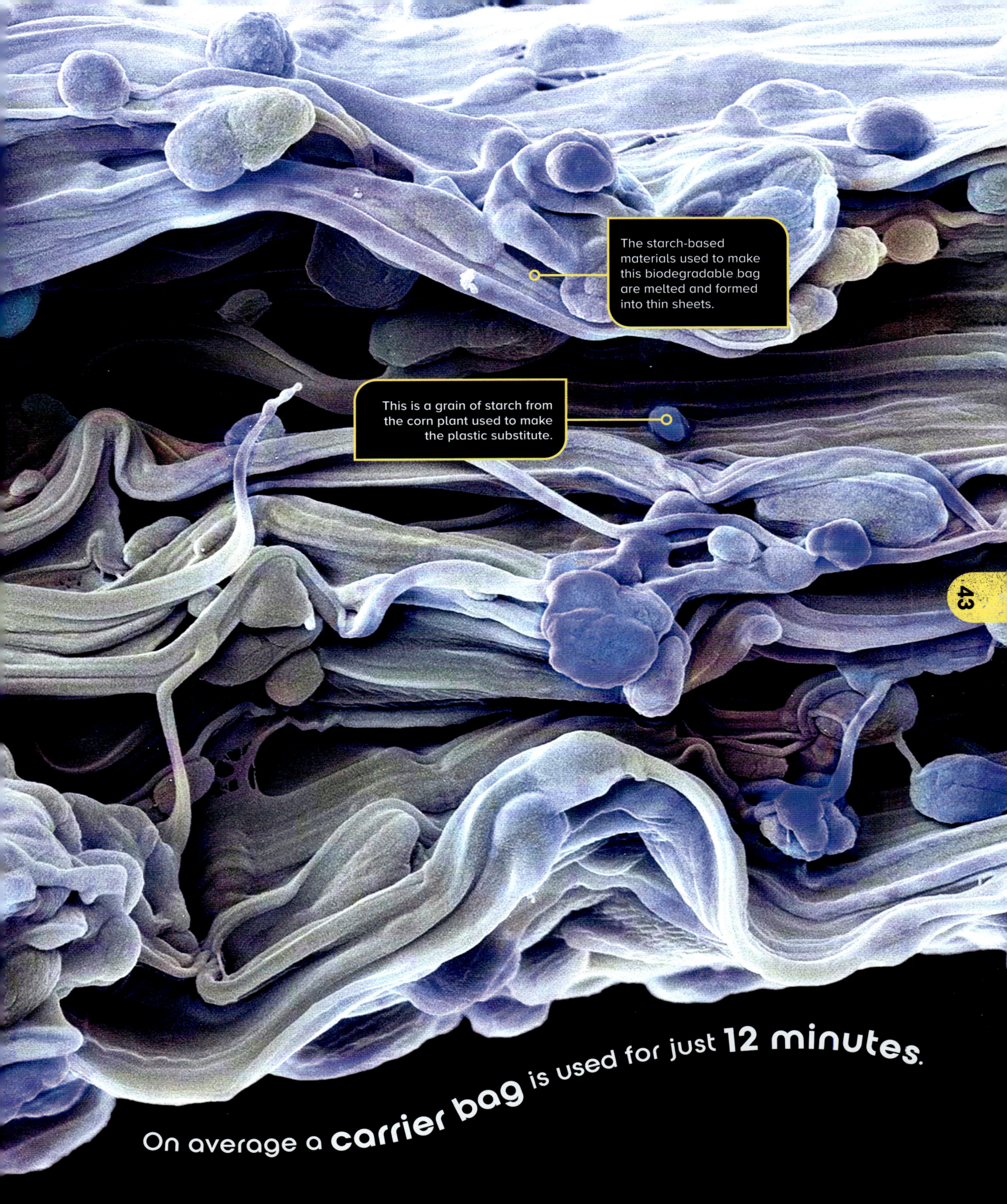

The starch-based materials used to make this biodegradable bag are melted and formed into thin sheets.

This is a grain of starch from the corn plant used to make the plastic substitute.

On average a **carrier bag** is used for just **12 minutes**.

Polystyrene cup

Disposable coffee cups are made of a super lightweight material that's 98 per cent air and only 2 per cent solid plastic. Called polystyrene foam, this material is great for keeping things warm and is also used to make takeaway food cartons and the insulation boards in the walls and floors of houses. However, this useful substance is very difficult to recycle and it crumbles into millions of tiny white bits of litter.

How it's made

Making polystyrene foam is like making popcorn. First, thousands of tiny beads of solid, clear plastic, each about 1 mm wide, are heated with steam. Heat makes a chemical mixed into the plastic turn to gas, blowing up each bead into a hollow ball 50 times larger. The foam balls are then put in moulds and heated again so they fuse together.

Polystyrene boards are made of foam beads stuck together.

Packing peanuts

Almost as light as air, polystyrene foam makes the perfect packing material as it adds little weight to parcels. Packing peanuts are designed to bounce about and absorb bumps. This creates static electricity, which is why they cling to you after you open a parcel.

A polystyrene cup can take 500 years to break down in the environment.

Single-use polystyrene cups are rarely recycled. Some countries have banned them.

Shock absorber

Polystyrene foam is a good shock absorber and is used to make bicycle helmets. In a crash, the foam gets squashed, which absorbs the energy of the impact and spreads the force over a wide area, reducing the chance of a head injury. After an impact, the helmet is no longer safe and should be replaced.

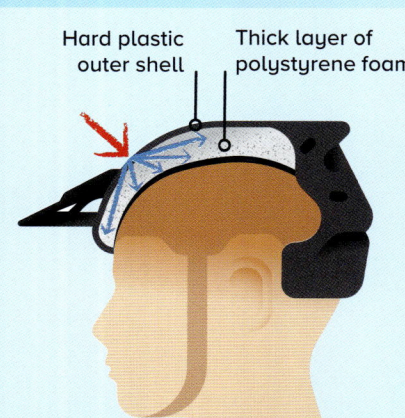

Hard plastic outer shell

Thick layer of polystyrene foam

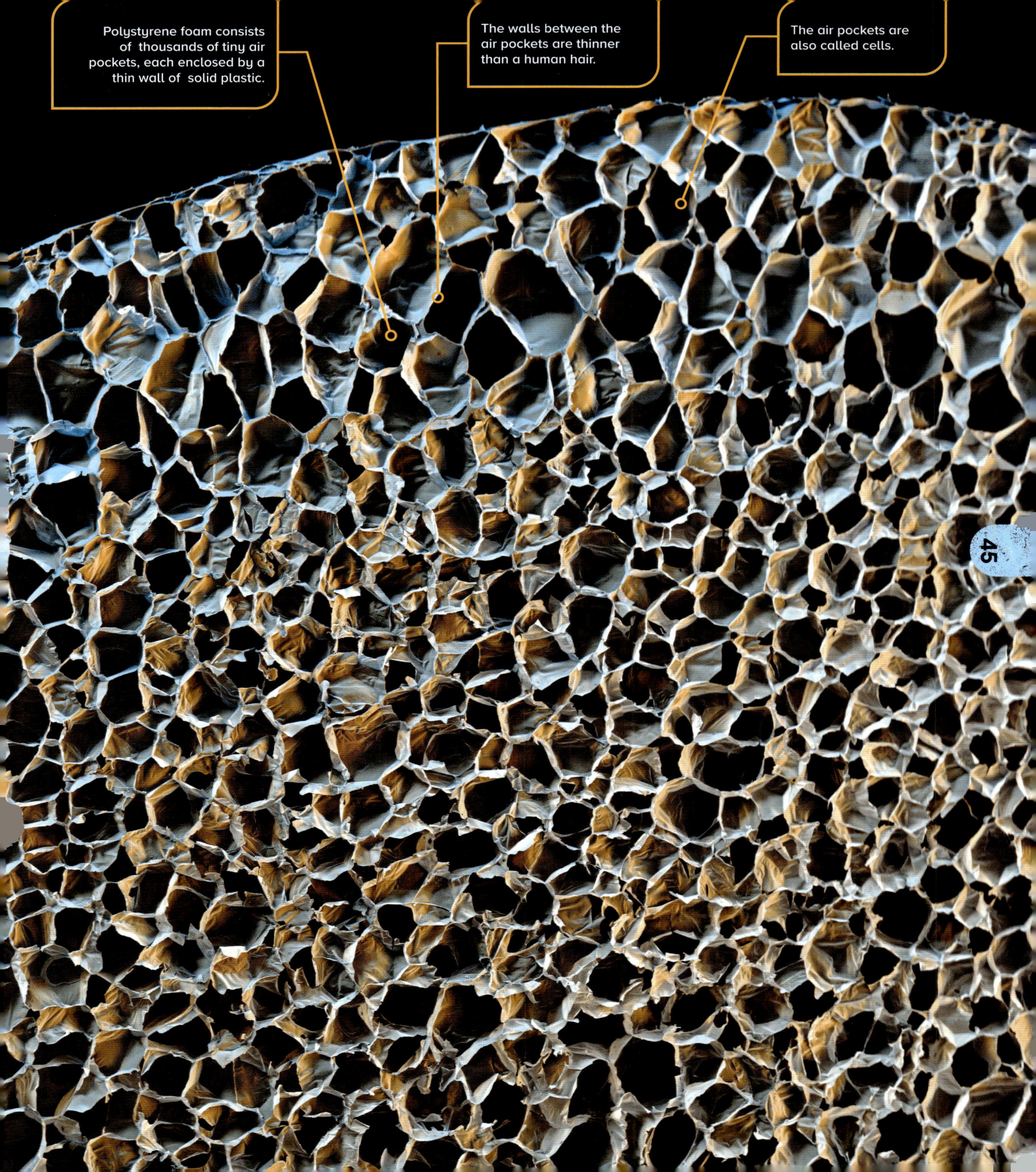

Polystyrene foam consists of thousands of tiny air pockets, each enclosed by a thin wall of solid plastic.

The walls between the air pockets are thinner than a human hair.

The air pockets are also called cells.

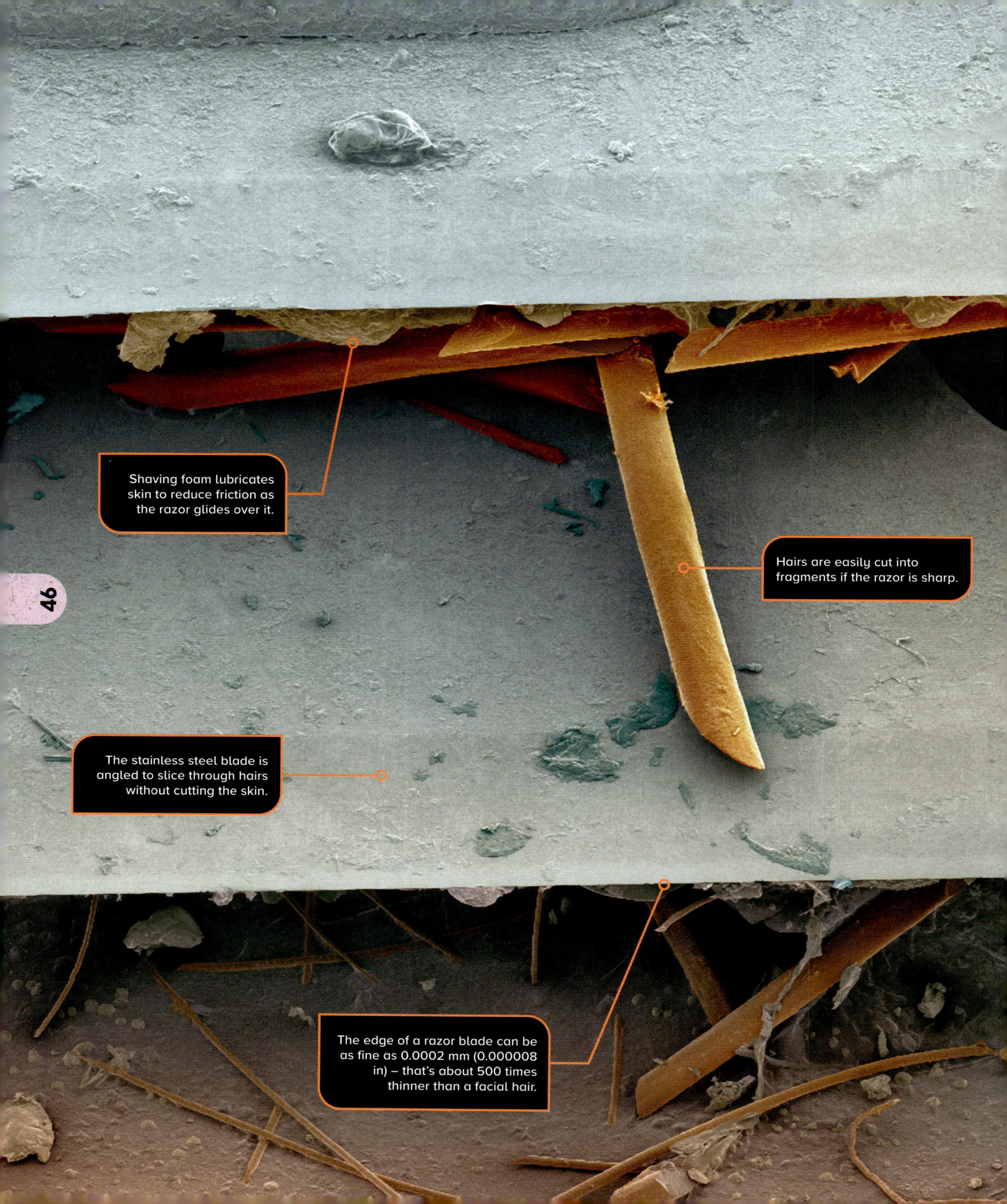

Razor blade

People use razors to remove unwanted hair. Modern razors often have two or more angled blades lined up in a cartridge (container), as seen in this close-up image. These multi-blade razors give very close shaves.

How it works: Multi-blade razor

In a multi-blade razor the blades work in sequence, one after the other, to cut hair. The first blade is angled to lift the hair as it cuts. Before it falls back, the second and third blades cut it again, giving a closer shave and smoother skin.

First blade
Hair is pushed up as it's cut
This cartridge contains three blades.

Prehistoric people used **flint, clam shells**, and even **shark teeth** as razors.

Flint
Clam shell
Shark tooth

Increasing the pressure

Blades cut because they concentrate a force into a very small area of contact, creating high pressure. A sharp blade has a very thin edge, making cutting easy. After repeated use, blades become blunt because the cutting edge wears down and forms a wider area of contact, which produces less pressure.

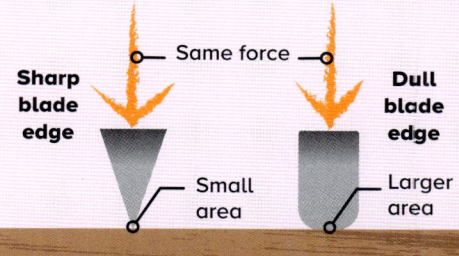

Same force
Sharp blade edge — Small area
Dull blade edge — Larger area

Reducing the pressure

Some objects work the opposite way to a razor blade. They spread the force over a larger surface area to reduce pressure. Snowshoes spread out the wearer's weight, preventing the person from sinking into snow.

Throwaway blade

Hair is up to 50 times softer than the razor blade cutting it. However, it can still damage a blade over time, by causing tiny cracks that grow into larger chips in the blade's edge. Once chipped, a blade is more likely to chip again. Most razor blades are designed to be thrown away once the blades are blunt.

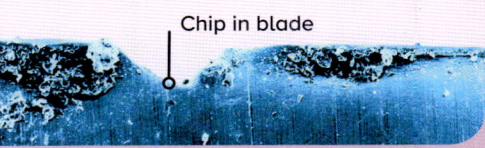

Chip in blade

How it works: Guitar string

A vibrating guitar string produces sound waves that travel through air. We detect and interpret these waves as sound. A string that vibrates fast produces high-frequency sound waves that we hear as high-pitched. A string that vibrates slowly produces low-frequency waves that we hear as a low-pitched (deep). The frequency of the sound waves in air matches the number of times a string vibrates back-and-forth in a second.

Changing pitch

Three factors affect the pitch of a vibrating guitar string: its gauge (thickness), tension (tightness), and length. Thicker strings make lower-pitched notes. Tuning pegs can alter the tension of the strings, making them tighter or looser. Tighter strings produce higher notes. The length of each string can be changed by the player pressing down on the string at different places along its length. The shorter the string's length, the higher the note.

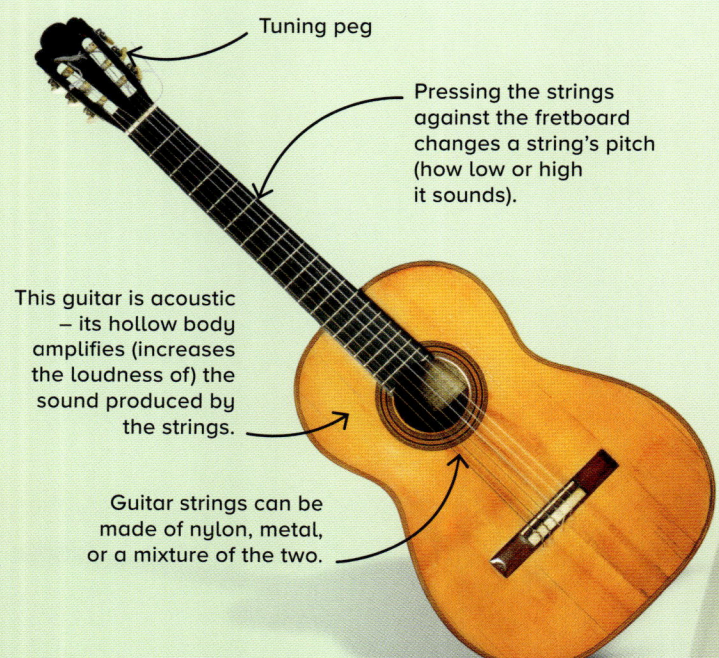

Tuning peg

Pressing the strings against the fretboard changes a string's pitch (how low or high it sounds).

This guitar is acoustic – its hollow body amplifies (increases the loudness of) the sound produced by the strings.

Guitar strings can be made of nylon, metal, or a mixture of the two.

Guitar string

Whether plucking a gentle melody or thrashing out loud chords, a guitar player uses the instrument's strings to make sounds. When played, the strings vibrate back and forth hundreds of times per second, moving the air to create sound waves. When viewed under a microscope, the many thin nylon strands that form a guitar string, wrapped by a coiled metal wire, can be seen.

Electric guitars

Unlike an acoustic guitar, an electric guitar's body does not amplify sound. Instead, an electric guitar has pickups – devices that convert the vibrations of the strings into an electrical signal. The signal travels to an amplifier, where it is converted into sound and played through a loudspeaker.

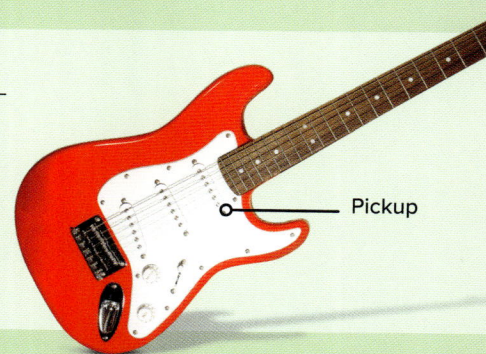

Pickup

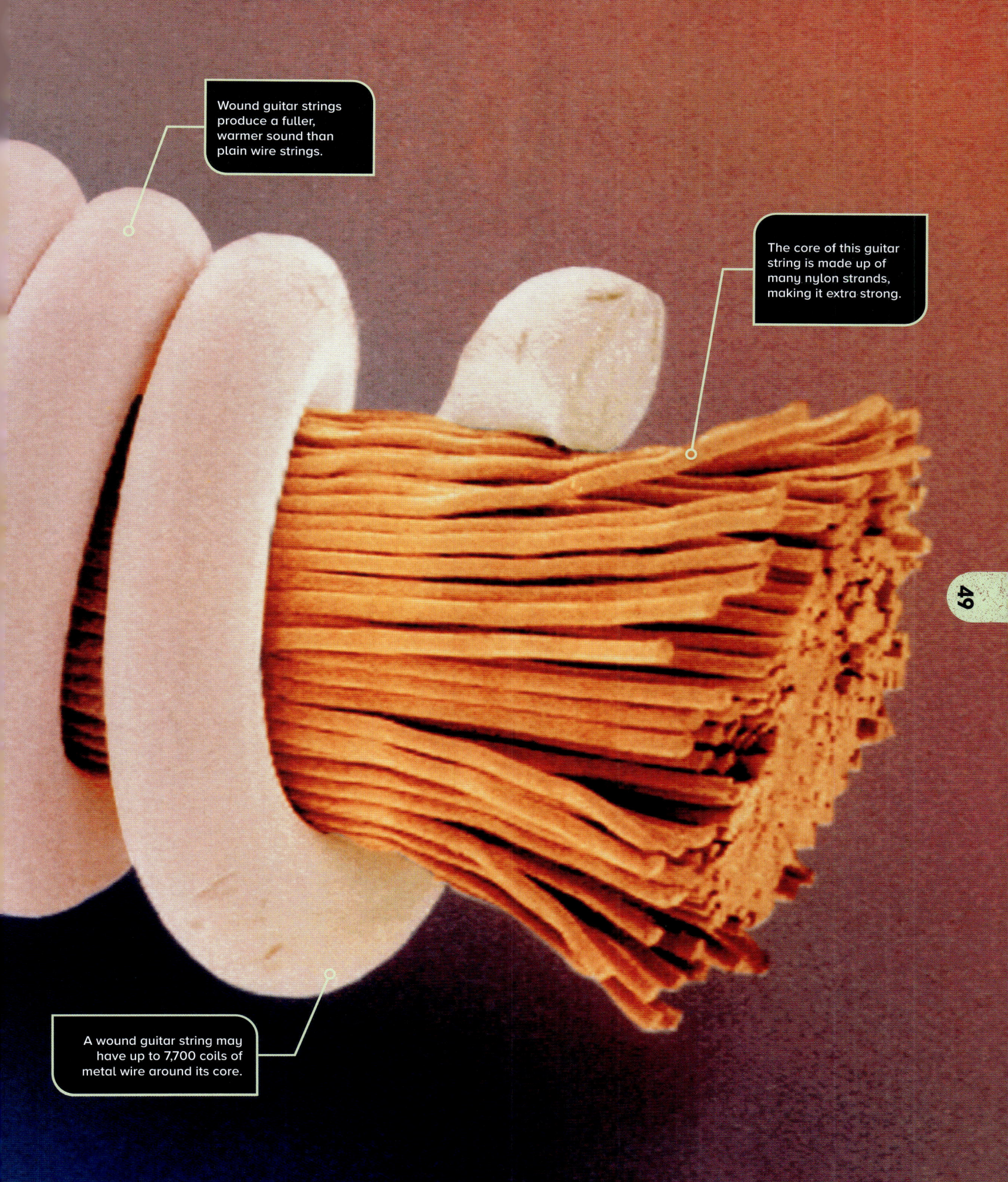

A dangerous history

In the 19th century, matches were made from white phosphorus, a toxic substance that caused the jawbones of many match industry workers to rot away. The use of white phosphorus in matches was banned as a result.

Matchstick

Strike a safety match and it almost instantly bursts into flame, but it happens so quickly and on a match head so small that it's almost impossible to see how it happened. Lighting a match involves a chemical reaction called combustion, which is triggered by heat generated from friction.

A regular-sized matchstick takes 10–15 seconds to burn down to the end.

A safety match head ignites at temperatures above 180°C (356°F) and may reach more than 1,500°C (2,732°F) as it burns.

What is friction?

Friction is a force that occurs when two objects rub together. Kinetic energy in the moving objects changes to heat energy. Things with rough surfaces usually produce more friction than smooth surfaces.

Brake pads press on wheel rim, creating friction

Helpful friction
Friction can be helpful. For example, squeezing the brake pads onto a bicycle wheel slows a bike down.

Bicycle chain

Unhelpful friction
Friction can also be unhelpful. Friction between a bicycle's chain and gears causes wear. It also wastes energy as heat if the parts aren't regularly oiled to help them move smoothly.

How it works: Matchstick

The friction created when a match is struck against a matchbox generates heat. This sets off a chemical reaction, which makes the match ignite (catch fire).

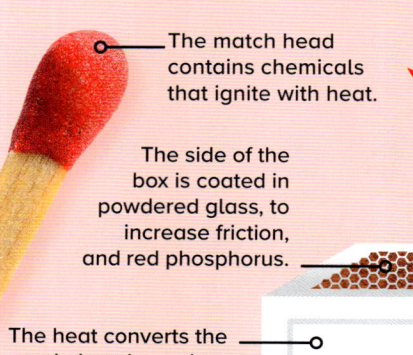

The match head contains chemicals that ignite with heat.

The side of the box is coated in powdered glass, to increase friction, and red phosphorus.

The heat converts the red phosphorus into white phosphorus, which reacts with chemicals in the match head that ignite.

Red phosphorus · Powdered glass

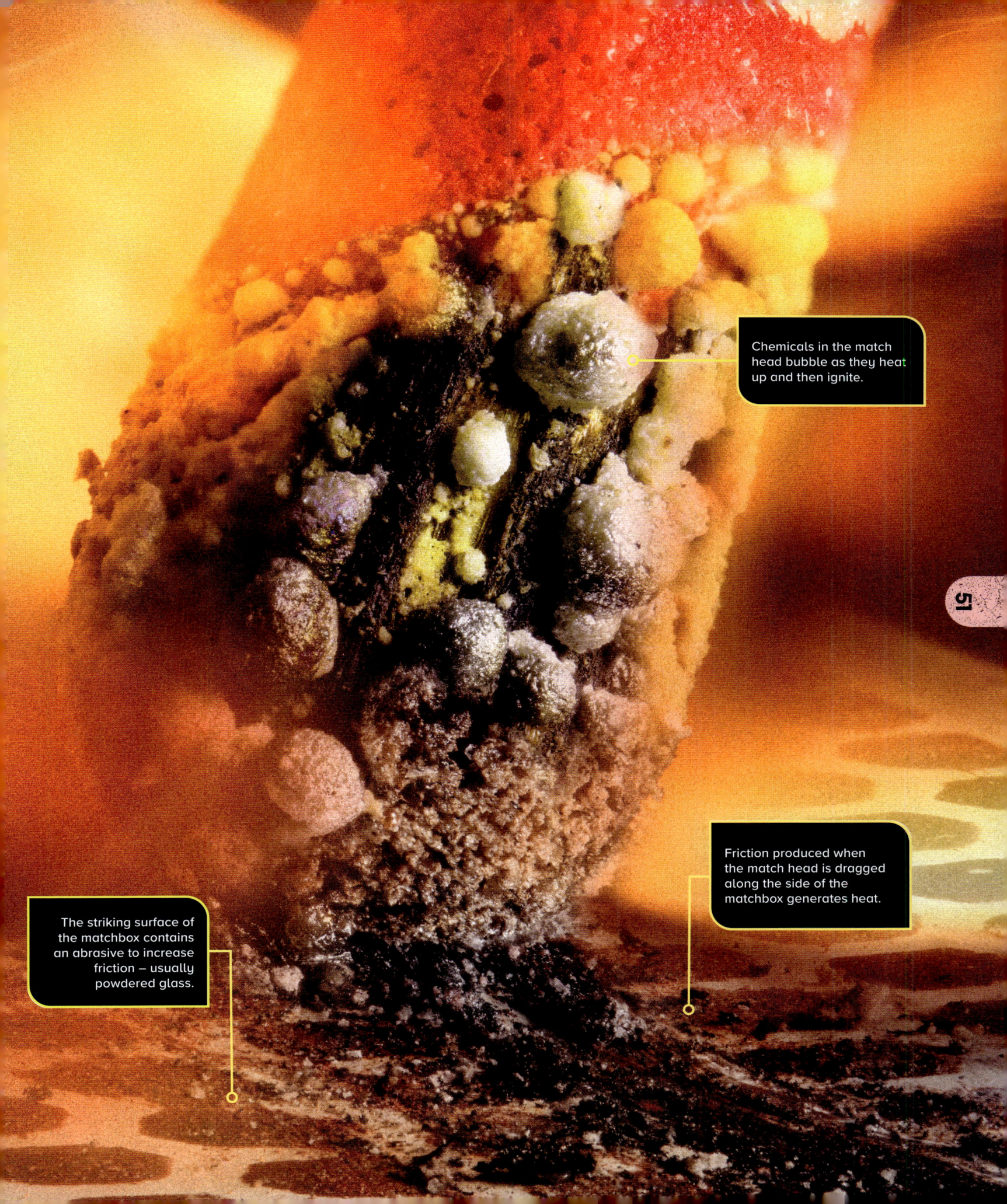

Chemicals in the match head bubble as they heat up and then ignite.

Friction produced when the match head is dragged along the side of the matchbox generates heat.

The striking surface of the matchbox contains an abrasive to increase friction – usually powdered glass.

51

Concrete

After water, the world's most used material is concrete. This super-strong building material is a mix of different materials bound together, as this microscope image shows. It can stay strong for centuries — some concrete structures built by the Romans 2,000 years ago are still standing today.

How it works: Concrete

Concrete is a mixture of cement, water, and aggregate (sand, gravel, and crushed stone). Cement is made from limestone and clay, which are heated together in an oven and then ground into a fine powder. When mixed with water, cement forms a paste that can bond with aggregate. This wet concrete mixture sets to become as hard as rock.

Crushed stone and gravel · Cement · Water · Sand

Compression and tension

Concrete has great compressive strength. This means it's good at resisting being compressed (squashed) by heavy loads placed on top of it, so it's often used to make vertical pillars. In contrast, concrete has far less tensile strength. It's not good at resisting being pulled or stretched, so horizontal beams under great tension may crack.

Bad at resisting tension · Load · Load · Tension · Compression · Good at resisting compression

Big pour

The world's largest concrete structure is the Three Gorges Dam in China. A total of 27 million cubic metres (950 million cubic feet) of concrete was used to build it — enough to fill 10,000 Olympic swimming pools. It also contains enough steel to build 63 Eiffel Towers.

The dam's concrete wall is 185 m (607 ft) high.

Reinforced concrete

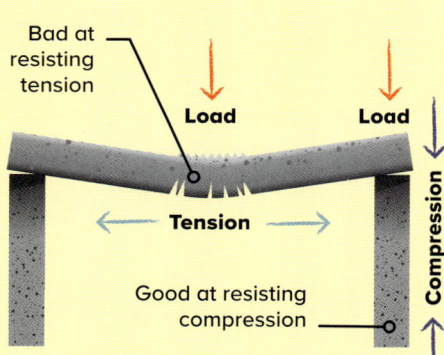

This type of concrete has steel rods added to it before it sets. The rods increase the concrete's tensile strength.

Around **30 billion tonnes** of concrete are used worldwide every year.

The Guggenheim building, New York

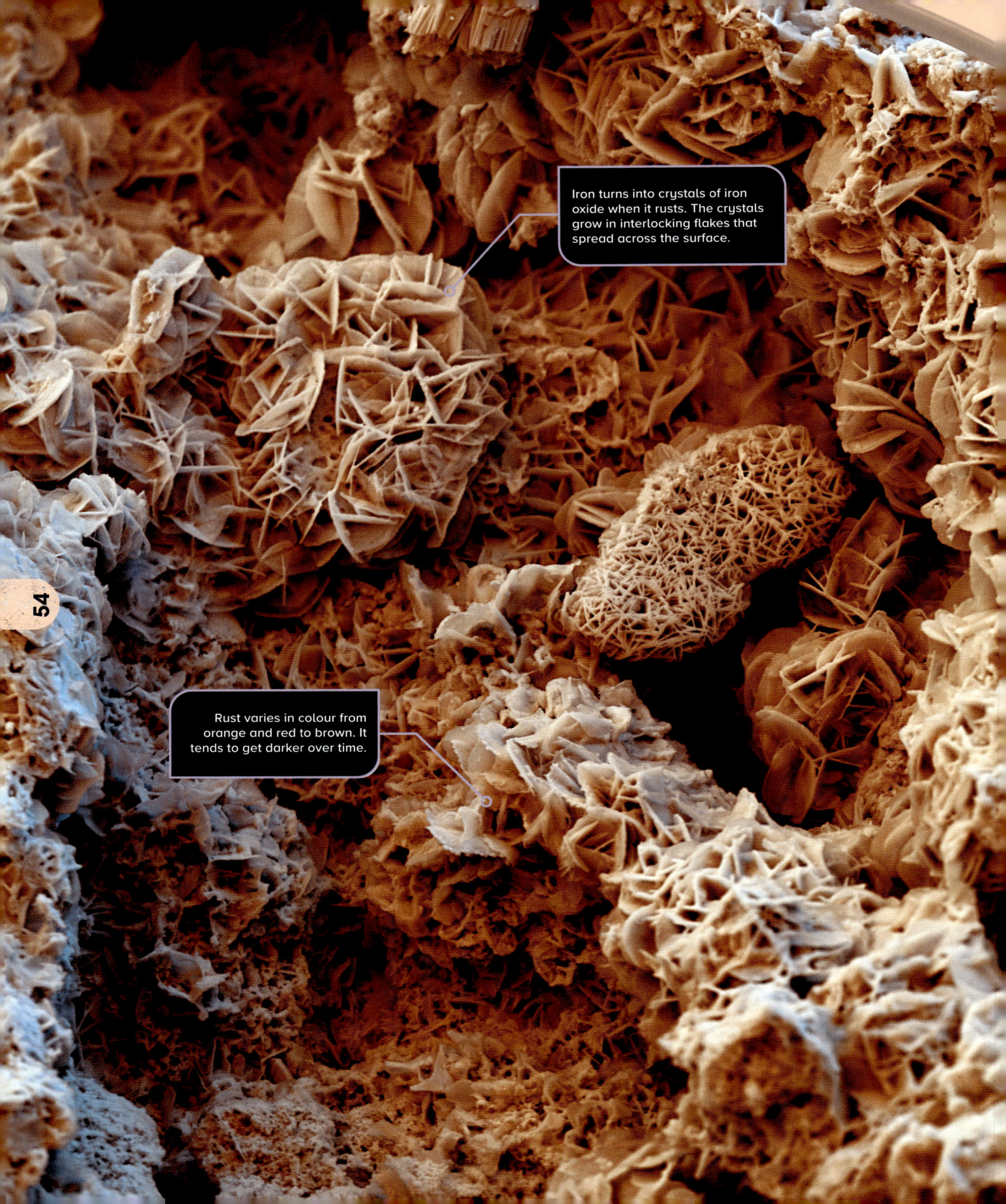

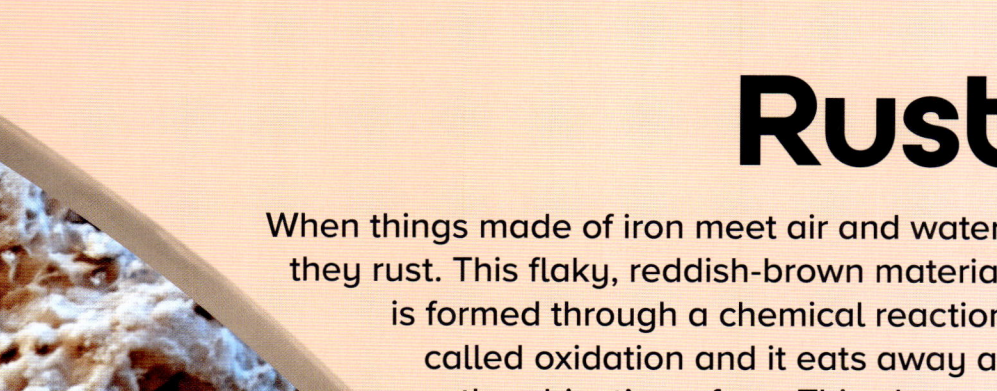

Rust

When things made of iron meet air and water, they rust. This flaky, reddish-brown material is formed through a chemical reaction called oxidation and it eats away at the object's surface. This electron microscope image shows rust magnified 7,000 times, revealing a forest of flaky iron oxide crystals.

Salt speeds up rusting, which is why **cars near the sea** rust **faster**.

How it works: Rusting

Iron turns into a compound called iron oxide when it rusts. This takes up more space than iron, so iron parts in buildings expand as they rust. The expansion can crack concrete or mortar, which may then crumble and fall off. Over time, rusting can make everything from cars and ships to bridges and skyscrapers fall to bits.

Preventing rust

Rust can be prevented by protecting the surface of iron or steel from water and oxygen. One way is to paint or grease it. Another is to cover it in a protective layer of a metal that doesn't rust, such as zinc. This is called galvanizing. Steel can also be made rust-resistant by combining it with other metals, such as chromium.

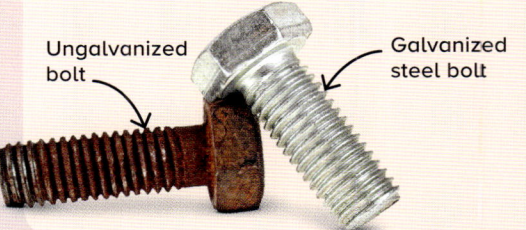

Ungalvanized bolt — Galvanized steel bolt

Rusty ships

The salt in seawater speeds up the chemical reaction that causes rusting, so boats made of steel (which is mostly iron) need constant care. This trawler has now rusted too much to be repaired and has been abandoned.

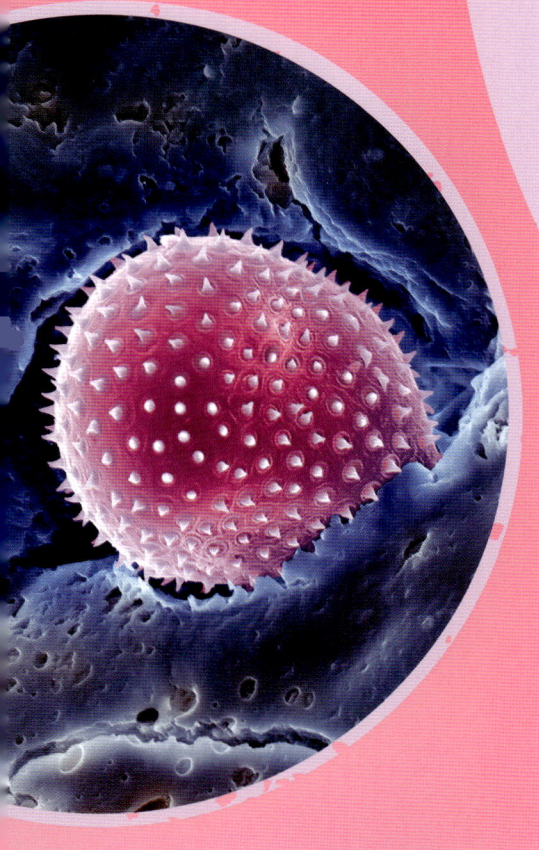

The human body

Blood

A single droplet of blood, just 1 mm (0.04 in) across, can contain more than 5 million red blood cells. They are so tiny that 50 of them can fit on the tip of an injection needle. Pumped around a network of blood vessels by the heart, red blood cells perform vital work, carrying oxygen to every part of the body.

How it works: Blood

Blood transports oxygen, nutrients, and waste products around the body. As well as red blood cells, it includes a watery, yellowish liquid called plasma, white blood cells to fight infection, and platelets, which help heal wounds.

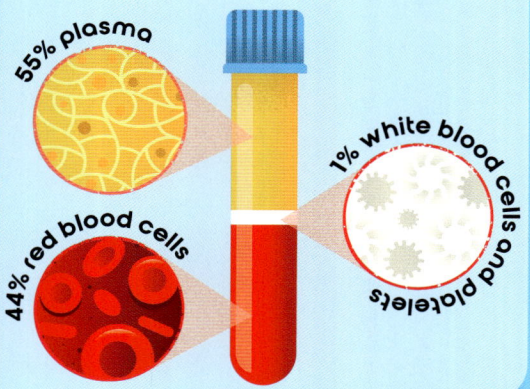

55% plasma
44% red blood cells
1% white blood cells and platelets

Red blood cells are smooth, flexible discs able to move easily through capillaries, the narrowest blood vessels.

The cell's shape, curved inwards on each side, increases its surface area to absorb more oxygen.

The body's defence system

White blood cells patrol the body hunting for harmful bacteria, viruses, and other microorganisms, which together are known as pathogens. There are different types of white blood cells, each with specialized jobs. Some types seek out and mark any potentially dangerous pathogens, while others are responsible for destroying them. White blood cells are bigger than red blood cells, but still so small that a single drop of blood can contain more than 25,000 of them.

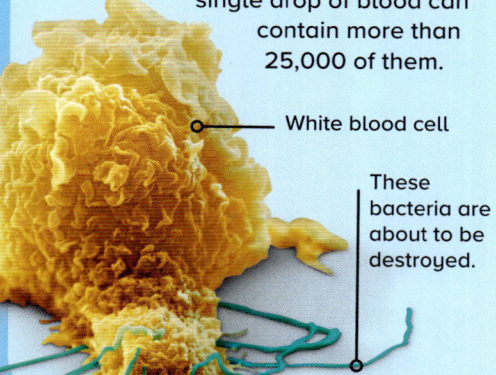

White blood cell

These bacteria are about to be destroyed.

A red blood cell can complete a journey around the body in less than a minute.

Healing wounds

When a blood vessel is cut, it narrows to slow the flow of leaking blood. Platelets in the blood become sticky. They clump together and attach to the vessel wall, temporarily plugging the leak. Long, sticky strands of a substance called fibrin start to grow, forming a mesh that acts like a net to trap red blood cells. The cells and fibrin harden (clot) to form a scab.

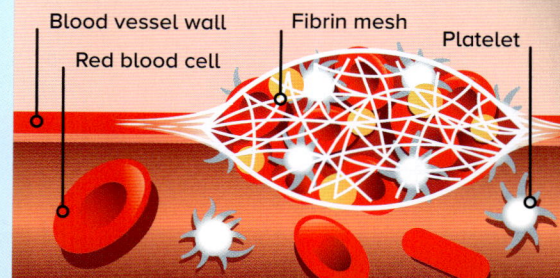

Blood vessel wall
Red blood cell
Fibrin mesh
Platelet

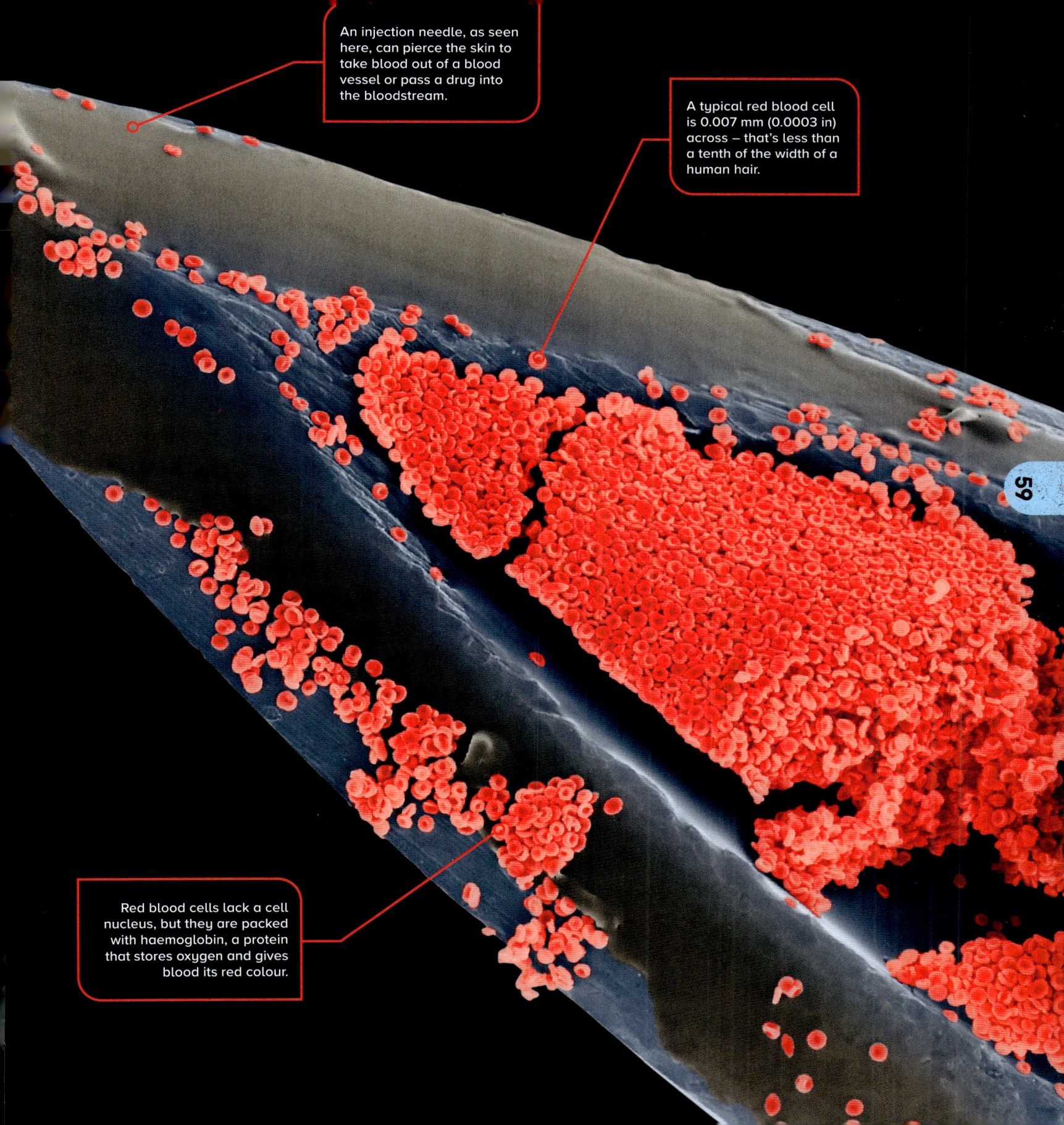

Skin

Our skin might feel smooth, but up close it looks like a rough landscape on an alien world. Skin is amazing stuff: it is waterproof, keeps germs out, bends and stretches as we move, and heals itself when damaged. It is also the body's largest organ. What you can see here is the skin's outer layer of cells, and each square centimetre (0.15 square inch) of your body has around 7 million of them.

How it works: Skin

Skin is made up of three layers. Each layer has a different function.

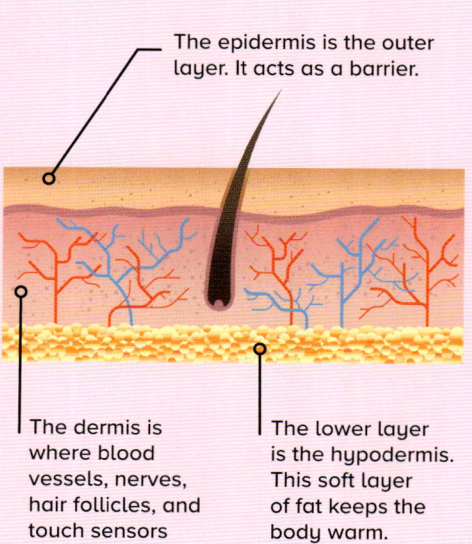

The epidermis is the outer layer. It acts as a barrier.

The dermis is where blood vessels, nerves, hair follicles, and touch sensors are located.

The lower layer is the hypodermis. This soft layer of fat keeps the body warm.

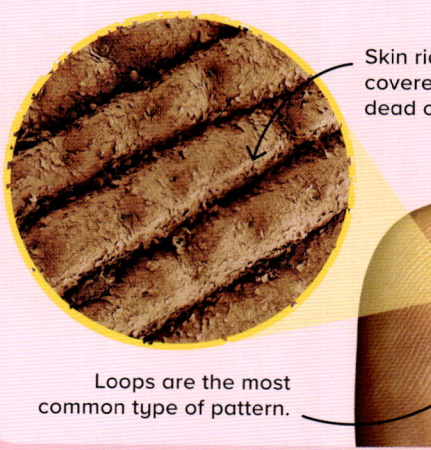

Skin ridges, covered in dead cells

Loops are the most common type of pattern.

Fingerprints

The skin on our hands, and especially our fingertips, has tiny ridges. These increase the skin's surface area and help us to grip objects. The ridges form loops, arches, and swirls, and everybody's fingers — even identical twins' — have a unique pattern. When we touch objects we leave behind a fingerprint made of oils and skin cells. These prints have long been used to identify criminals.

Your skin is thinnest on your eyelids and thickest on the soles of your feet.

Nails grow at a rate of 3 mm (0.11 in) a month, taking six months to be replaced entirely.

Fingernails

Keratin, the protein that makes skin tough, is also found in fingernails. Other animals use the same stuff to make their scales, feathers, hooves, horns, and claws. Nails grow from the skin at the base of the nail. New cells push the nail body (the visible part) forwards, filling with keratin as they do so.

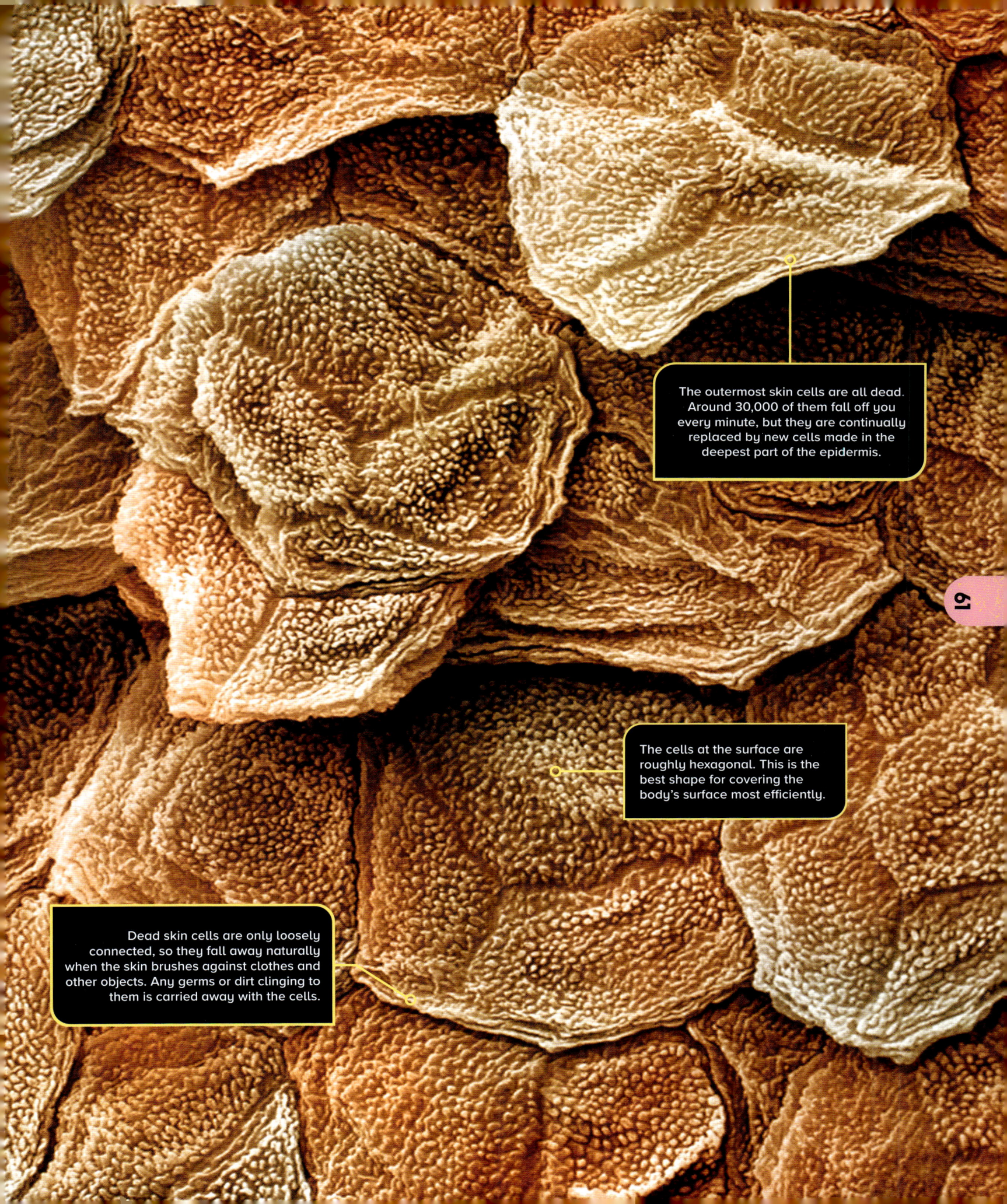

Sweat pore

Our skin is covered in millions of tiny openings known as sweat pores. Each pore leads to a sweat gland below the surface of the skin. When you get warm the sweat glands kick into action, producing sweat, which helps cool the body down as it evaporates off the skin. This electron microscope image shows a sweat pore on a hand magnified around 6,000 times.

Your body has 2–4 million sweat pores.

How it works: Sweat pore

There are two main types of sweat glands. Eccrine glands are the most common, found all over the body. Apocrine glands are mainly located in the armpits and groin.

Eccrine glands empty directly onto the skin surface.

Apocrine gland produces a thicker, oily sweat as we get older. The gland empties sweat into a hair follicle.

Hair follicle

Eccrine gland produces the watery sweat that helps us regulate our body temperature.

Does sweat smell?

Sweat itself doesn't smell. Body odour only develops after skin bacteria start to feed on the organic matter in sweat – especially the sweat from apocrine glands. Bacteria thrive in the warm, moist areas where apocrine glands are found. As they digest the nutrients in sweat, the bacteria release waste chemicals that we can smell.

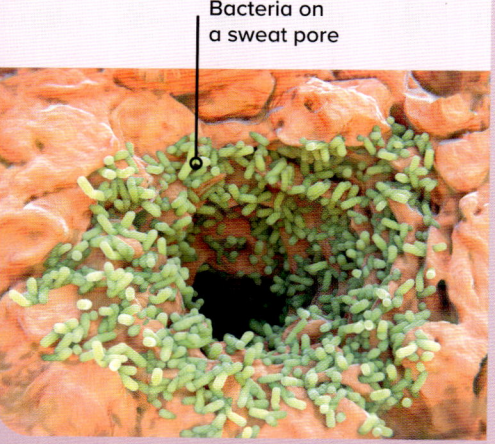

Bacteria on a sweat pore

Who sweats and who doesn't?

Horses and humans both sweat to cool down, but most other animals do not have sweat glands. They use other ways to keep cool.

Cats lick their fur and cool down as the saliva evaporates.

Elephants lose heat through their ears and spray themselves with water.

Pigs roll in wet mud, cooling as the water evaporates. Mud is also a sunscreen.

Dogs pant, increasing the evaporation of water from their mouth and lungs.

Tongue spreads out to increase surface area

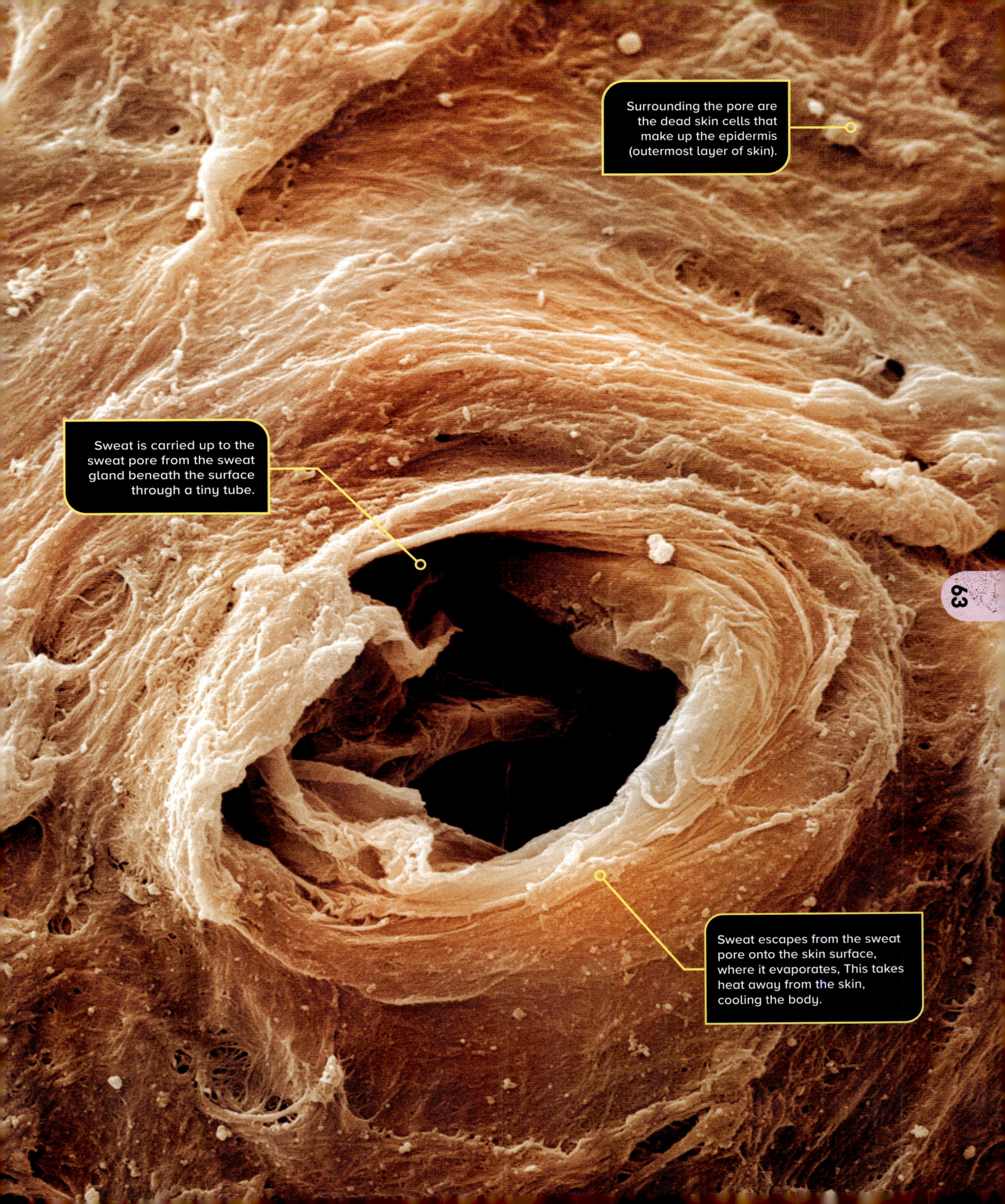

Nose

Sticky snot

Snot has a very important job. This sticky substance helps to keep your nose clean, by trapping dirt, dust, and germs, and preventing them from getting into your lungs. It also helps to keep the inside of your nose moist. Snot is about 95 per cent water. The remaining 5 per cent is made up of substances that give it its slimy texture.

Your nose is the main entrance to your airways – it protects your lungs from dirt, dust, and germs, and very cold or very hot air. When you breathe in, a thin layer of mucus (snot) moistens the air and catches any unwanted particles – such as this pollen grain, shown magnified 5,700 times.

Your nose makes four large glasses of snot every day.

Hairy defence

Tiny hairs, called cilia, line your nose and airways. They waft together in rhythmic waves to sweep snot and trapped particles from the nose into the throat, where they can be swallowed or spat out. This scanning electron microscopic image shows a thick layer of cilia lining the nasal cavity.

No need for noses

Some animals don't have noses. They detect smells with other parts of their bodies. Moths like this silk moth use their antennae, which are covered in odour receptors. Males have the most odour receptors, to help them search for a female mate.

How it works: Smell

When you breathe in through your nostrils, you inhale odour molecules – chemicals that float in the air and create smells. They travel into your nasal cavity, a large, air-filled space behind the nose. These molecules dissolve into the cavity's moist lining, where they are detected by receptor cells. Each receptor cell is connected to the olfactory bulb. Here, information about the odour molecules is processed before it is sent to the brain to identify the smell.

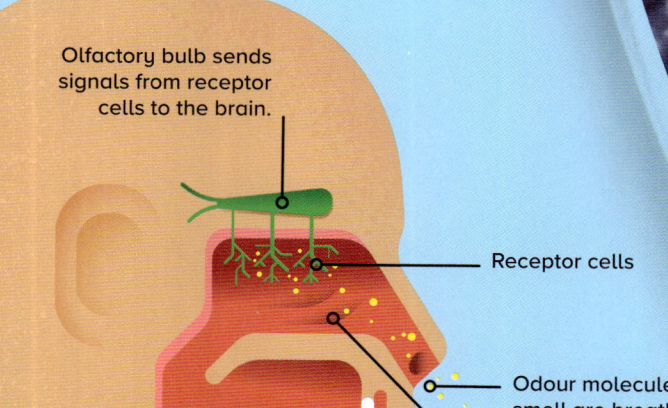

Olfactory bulb sends signals from receptor cells to the brain.

Receptor cells

Odour molecules from smell are breathed in.

Nasal cavity

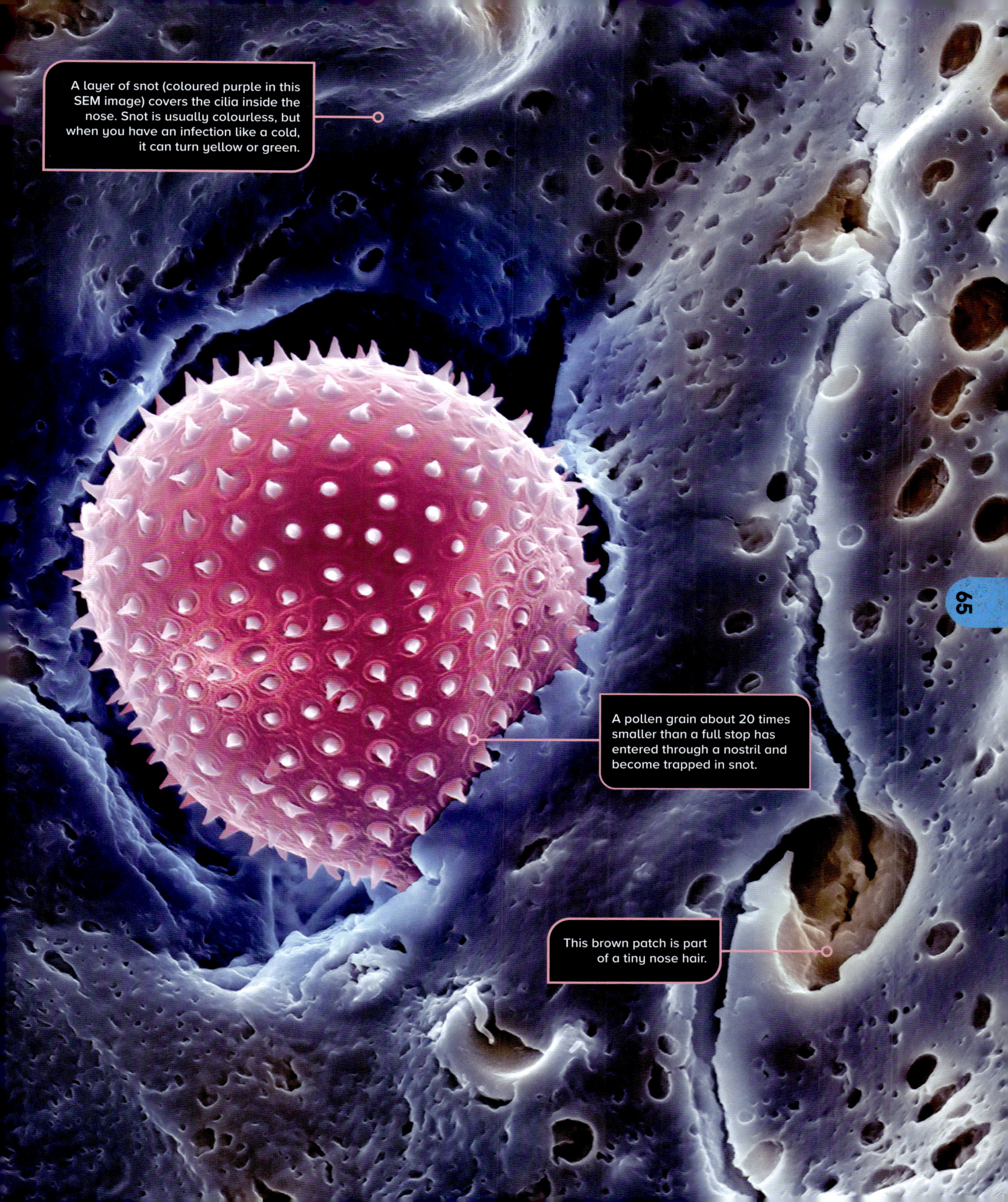

Parts of the eye

Light enters the eye through the pupil and is focused by the lens onto the retina at the back of the eye. Here, millions of light-sensitive cells convert light into electrical signals. These signals are sent to the brain by the optic nerve, a tightly packed bundle of more than a million nerve fibres. The brain processes these signals, and interprets them as images.

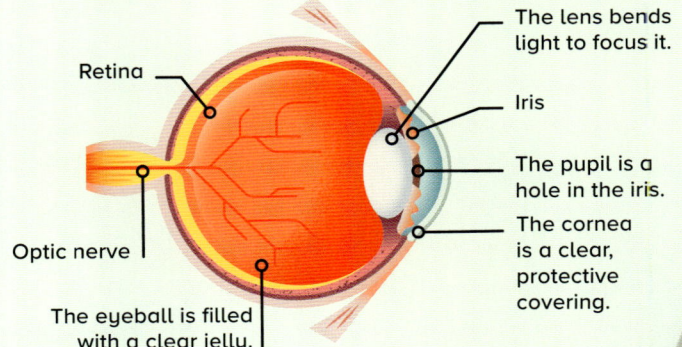

Iris

The coloured part of the human eye is called the iris. This circle of tiny muscles surrounds the pupil and can change shape to make the pupil larger or smaller, controlling how much light enters your eyes. Your irises also react to emotion. When you're excited, angry, or see something you like, your irises react and your pupils expand.

How it works: The iris

In bright light, your pupils shrink to stop you being dazzled. When it's dark, they widen to help you see. At their largest, they let in 20 times more light than at their smallest size. Two sets of muscles (circular and radial) in the iris contract (squeeze) or relax to adjust the pupil's size. You have no conscious control over them – it's an automatic reflex.

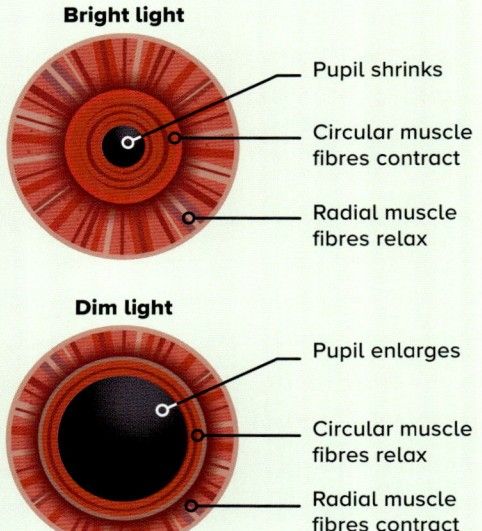

Every iris has a **different pattern** of **colours, ridges** and **wrinkles**, making each eyeball **unique**.

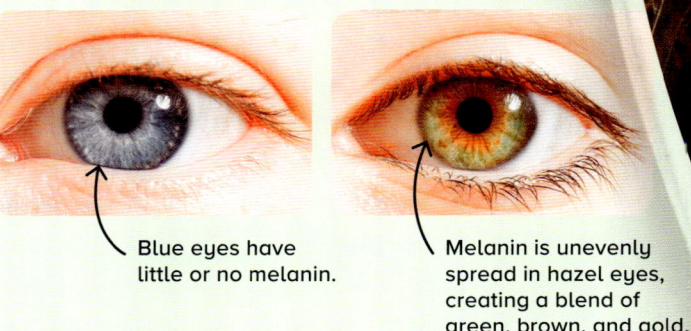

Eye colour

Your eye colour is determined by the amount of a substance called melanin in your iris. The more melanin, the darker the colour. More than 70 per cent of people have brown eyes. Less common colours include blue, hazel, green, and grey. Some people have two differently coloured irises – a condition called heterochromia.

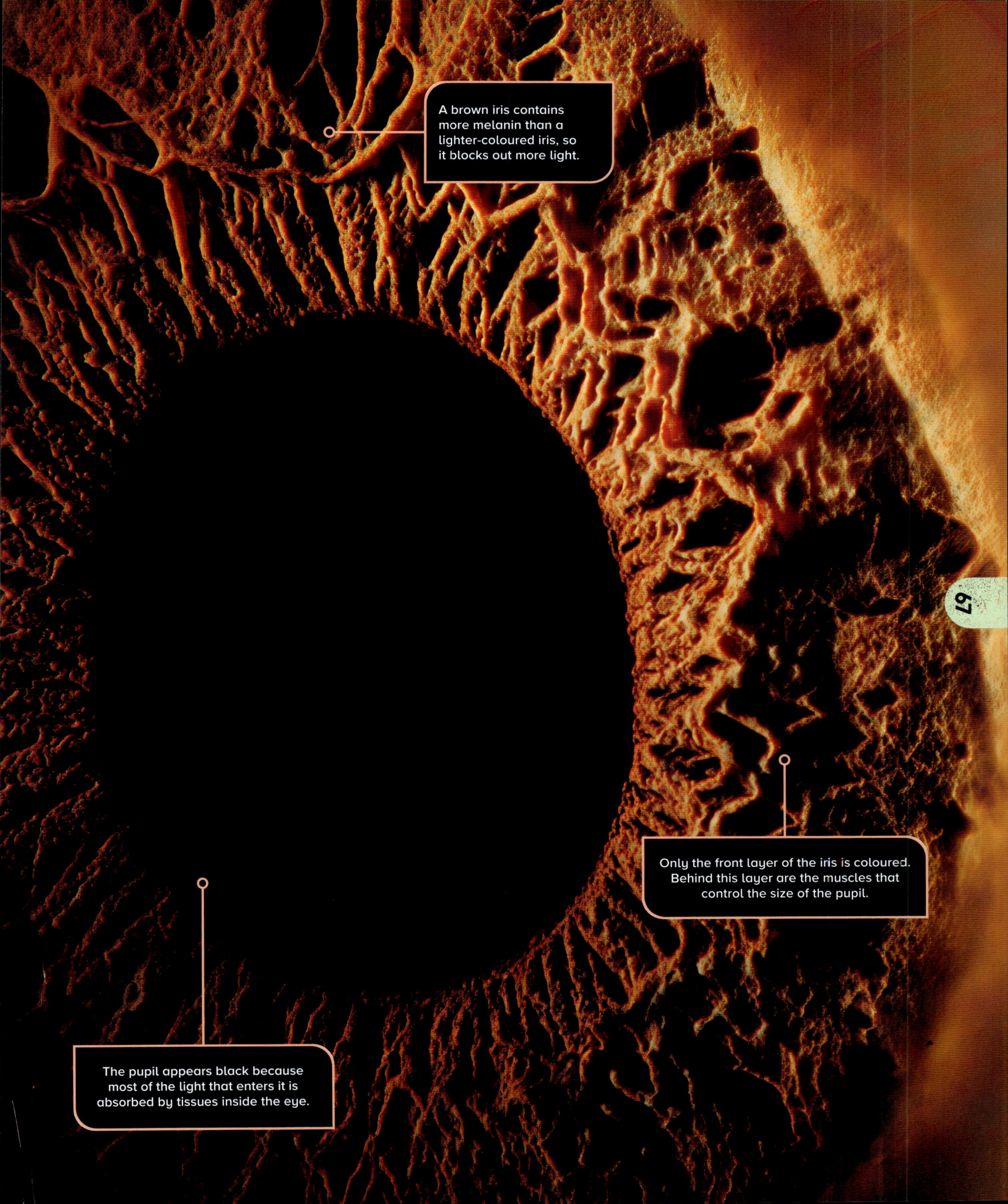

A brown iris contains more melanin than a lighter-coloured iris, so it blocks out more light.

Only the front layer of the iris is coloured. Behind this layer are the muscles that control the size of the pupil.

The pupil appears black because most of the light that enters it is absorbed by tissues inside the eye.

Hair

You **lose** around 100 hairs from your scalp every day.

About 96 per cent of your body is covered in hair – millions of them. Only the palms of your hands, the soles of your feet, and your lips are hairless. Hair grows from very small pits, known as follicles, in the skin. This close-up image shows the follicles of a person's scalp.

How it works: Hair follicle

An adult has around 5 million hair follicles on their body, which extend down into the lower layer of skin, the dermis. Most hair follicles contain a single shaft of hair that sticks out from the skin. Tiny blood vessels connect to the base of the follicle, supplying the hair with nutrients and oxygen for it to grow. An oily substance called sebum flows into the follicle from the oil gland. Sebum helps to keep the hair and nearby skin hydrated, and defends the body against bacteria.

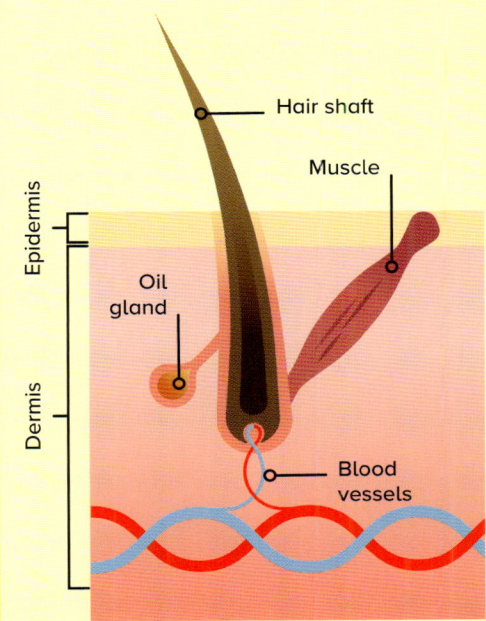

Types of hair

Whether you have straight, wavy, or curly hair depends on the shape of your hair follicles. They mould your hair as it grows.

Round follicle
Straight hair

Oval follicle
Wavy hair

Flat follicle
Curly hair

What is hair made from?

Hair is made from a tough substance called keratin, just like skin and nails. Keratin is a dead material, which is why it doesn't hurt when you get a haircut. A hair grows because new living cells are constantly being added to its root. As they form, they push older cells above them up and out of the skin. Further from their blood supply, the older cells die and harden as they fill with keratin.

Cross-section of hair

- The **cortex** contains keratin and melanin, which gives hair its colour.
- The **medulla** is the hair's hollow inner core.
- The **cuticle** is the outer layer – it is formed of overlapping dead cells.

Goosebumps

When you're feeling cold or scared, you might have noticed the hairs on your arms stand upright. Known as goosebumps, it happens because tiny muscles attached to the base of each hair follicle contract (squeeze), pulling the hair upright. Early humans had thicker hair than us, and when raised, the hairs would have trapped air that helped to keep them warm.

How it works: Head lice life cycle

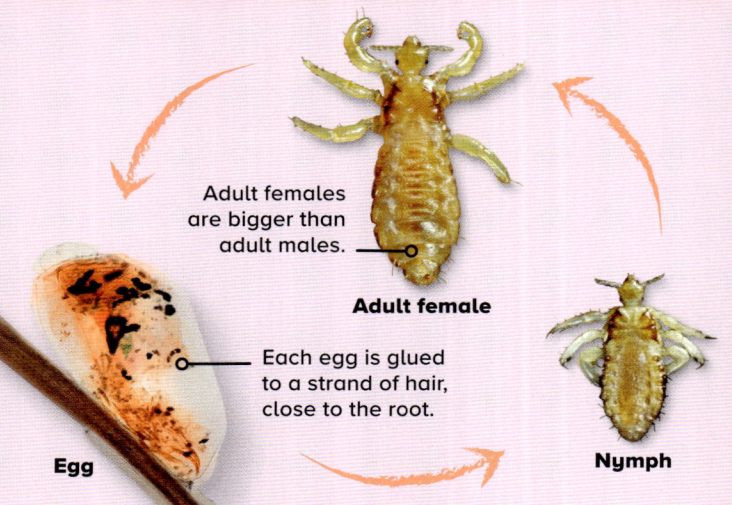

Adult females are bigger than adult males.

Adult female

Each egg is glued to a strand of hair, close to the root.

Egg

Nymph

An adult female head louse can lay up to six eggs a day. Eggs hatch in 6–10 days, each releasing a bloodthirsty nymph that needs a meal of blood within minutes to survive. Over the next 10 days, nymphs moult three times, shedding their exoskeleton as they grow. If removed from its host, a head louse will usually die within a day.

Eyelash mites

Microscopic mites may be hiding in your eyelashes. This image, magnified 190 times, shows their tails poking out from the base of an eyelash. In small numbers they're harmless, emerging at night to feast on dead skin and grease. However, they can cause a rash if there are too many.

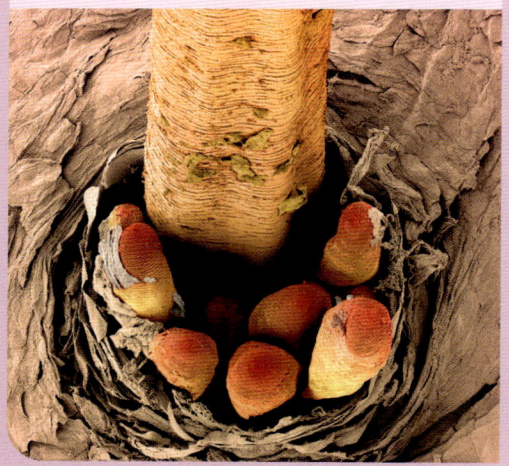

Head lice

These hard-to-spot insects, each about the size of a sesame seed, are parasites that can be hard to get rid of once they've moved in. Fast movers, they crawl through human hair, only stopping to bite their host's scalp and feed on blood. They don't spread disease, but their bites can be itchy. This electron microscope image shows one magnified about 100 times.

Other parasites

Many other mini creatures like to live on or inside us. Most are harmless or helpful like eyelash mites, while others can cause problems, from annoying itchy head lice to the three shown here, which can cause serious illness.

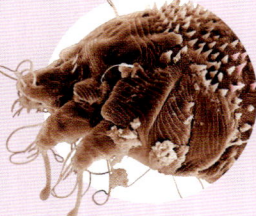

Scabies mites burrow under skin to lay their eggs.

Tapeworms live in the intestines and feed on foods eaten by their hosts.

Blood flukes invade blood vessels, causing serious illness.

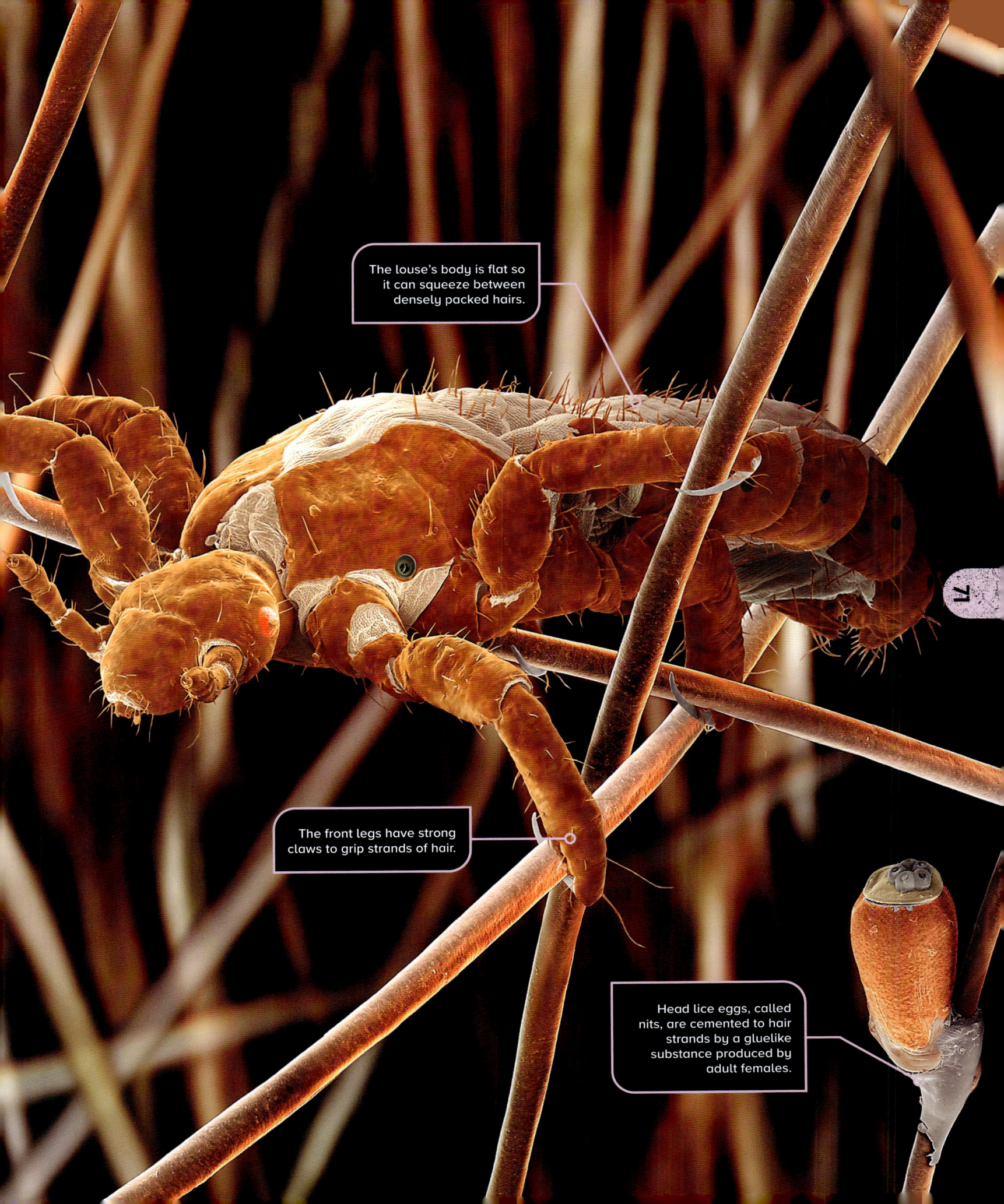

The louse's body is flat so it can squeeze between densely packed hairs.

The front legs have strong claws to grip strands of hair.

Head lice eggs, called nits, are cemented to hair strands by a gluelike substance produced by adult females.

What's a tooth made of?

The outermost layer of a tooth is made of enamel – the hardest substance in the human body, even stronger than bone. The enamel has sharp ridges and cusps (points) that grip and tear food when you bite and chew. Under the enamel is a bonelike material called dentine, which also forms the tooth's root. Dentine acts as a shock absorber while you chew.

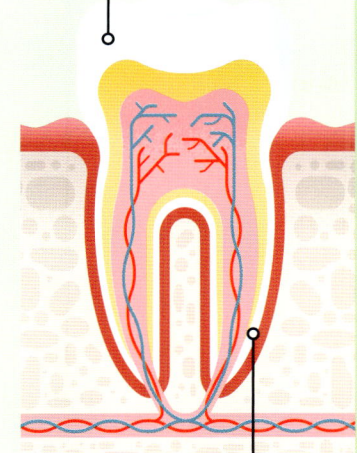

The crown is the top part of the tooth.

Each tooth is anchored deep into the jawbone by its root.

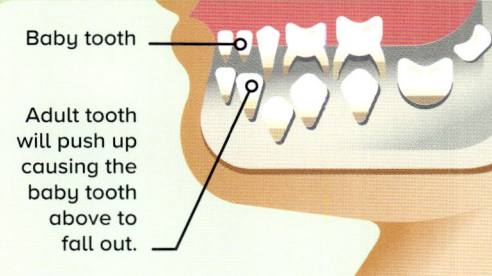

Baby tooth

Adult tooth will push up causing the baby tooth above to fall out.

Changing teeth

A set of 20 baby teeth emerge from the gums about 6–12 months after birth. These baby teeth start to fall out from age six onwards. They're eventually replaced by a set of 32 permanent adult teeth, with different types for biting, tearing, chewing, and grinding.

The average person spends two months of their life cleaning their teeth.

Teeth

Our teeth are essential for chewing and chomping food into smaller pieces to make it easier to swallow and digest. The biggest threat to healthy teeth is microscopic bacteria, which can cause tooth decay. More bacteria live inside a person's mouth than there are people on Earth, so keeping up with them is a challenge. The solution is to brush your teeth twice a day, every day.

What is tooth decay?

Tooth decay is caused by plaque – a sticky substance formed of saliva, food, and bacteria – that builds up on teeth. Bacteria in the plaque feed on leftover food particles, producing acid as a waste product. This acid eats away at the teeth, causing holes to form. If the acid reaches the pulp, it can cause toothache.

Each person's plaque can contain more than 200 different species of bacteria.

Ancient toothpaste

The ancient Romans made toothpastes from honey, charcoal, human urine, and even powdered mouse skulls. Today's toothpastes often include fluoride, which strengthens enamel and slows acid production by bacteria.

Honey

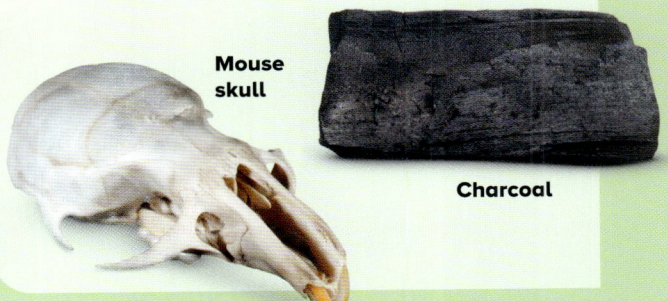

Mouse skull

Charcoal

Sitting in an opening called a taste pore, the top of a taste bud is exposed to chemicals from food.

Filiform papillae help grip food as you chew and move the food around your mouth.

Every person has their own pattern and number of papillae and taste buds, giving them a unique "tongue-print".

Tongue

Your tongue is not one but eight muscles combined, allowing it to move in ways that help you speak, taste, chew, and swallow. The tongue's outer surface is rough, covered in thousands of tiny bumps called papillae — as seen in this highly magnified image. Many of these papillae contain taste buds.

The tongue grows a new surface every 10 days.

How it works: Taste bud

Our sense of taste depends on taste buds — tiny balls of cells dotted around the tongue and rest of the mouth. We have 5000–10,000 taste buds, each less than a tenth of a millimetre (0.004 in) wide and containing around 100 taste receptor cells. These cells detect chemicals from food after they dissolve in saliva. The cells then send electrical signals to the brain, which interprets them as different tastes.

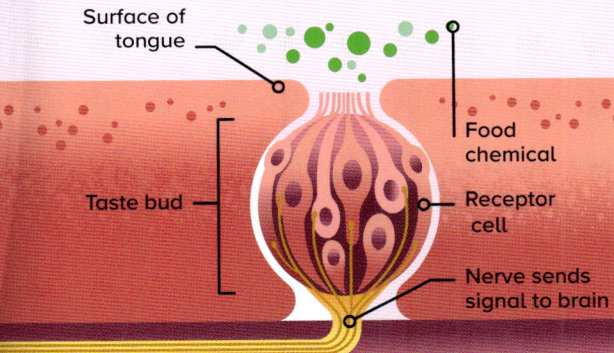

- Surface of tongue
- Food chemical
- Taste bud
- Receptor cell
- Nerve sends signal to brain

Tastes

We can only detect a limited number of tastes with our mouths — sour, sweet, salty, bitter, and umami (savoury). The countless different flavours of food come from a combination of the five tastes and also from our noses, which detect thousands of different odours when we eat or drink.

Sour · Sweet · Salty · Bitter · Umami

Foods rich in umami include meat, cheese, and mushrooms.

Hot stuff

Chilli peppers taste fiery because they contain a chemical called capsaicin. We don't taste capsaicin with our taste buds. Instead, it triggers pain and temperature receptors in the mouth, creating a burning sensation.

The Carolina Reaper is more than 1,000 times hotter than an average supermarket chilli.

Body bacteria

The human body has about 30 trillion cells — human cells, that is. There are even more (around 39 trillion) cells of bacteria and other microorganisms living on and inside your body. Some of them live on the skin, but most are in your digestive system. They are tiny — far too small to see with the naked eye — but can be seen under a microscope. These bacteria are living in a dollop of human poo.

How it works: Body bacteria

Bacteria feast on the nutrients in the gut. As they feed, they create gases and other chemicals that give poo its unpleasant smell. But while we provide bacteria with food and shelter, they also help us in return. Some of them break down foods that our digestive systems can't handle, providing us with important nutrients. Friendly bacteria also cover the lining of our gut, protecting it from harmful bacteria that cause diseases and food poisoning.

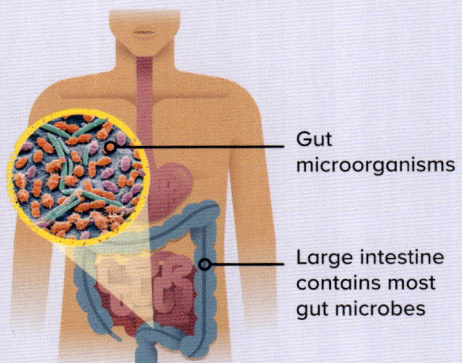

- Gut microorganisms
- Large intestine contains most gut microbes

What's poo made of?

Poo is mostly bacteria and water. The bacteria feed on the food we don't digest, on cells shed by our intestines, and on each other. The colour of poo comes from a yellowish fluid our bodies make to aid digestion. Bacteria turn this brown inside the large intestine.

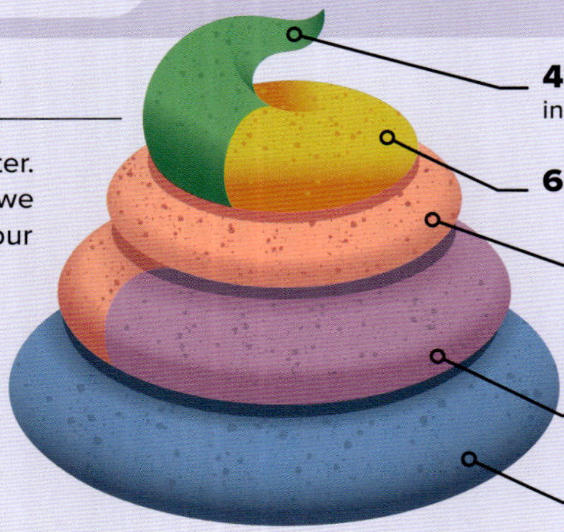

- **4% human cells** from the inside wall of the intestines.
- **6% fibre** from undigested food.
- **25% live bacteria** and other microbes. A teaspoon of poo can contain up to 5 billion viruses.
- **25% dead bacteria** and other microbes.
- **40% water** and minerals.

What's that smell?

Bacteria are the main reason we make bad smells. Microorganisms in the gut produce hydrogen sulphide gas, which gives farts that rotten-egg smell. Feet get stinky because of skin bacteria that feed on sweat, producing a cheesy-smelling acid. Bad breath, or halitosis, is caused by bacteria in the mouth that release sulphurous gases that smell like garlic and cabbage.

These bacteria cause stinky feet.

An average human poo has **50 times** more bacteria than there are **stars in our galaxy.**

The bacteria are mixed in with the solid fragments of food waste left behind by the human digestive system.

The average bacterium is about a thousandth the width of a human hair.

The natural world

Raindrops

When it rains, falling droplets of water collide and stick together, growing in size. The force of the air below the droplets flattens them into bun shapes and then hollow bell shapes as the drops get larger. Then they burst into a shower of tiny droplets and the cycle starts again.

Water

At the scale of a small insect, water behaves in ways that can seem very strange. A raindrop is harmless to us but a deadly hazard to an insect. Water sticks to itself with a force and creates a skin at its surface that insects can find challenging to break through, as seen in this close-up of a flat bug trapped in a raindrop.

How it works: Surface tension

A water molecule contains both positive and negative electrical charges. Since opposite charges attract each other, water molecules pull on each other in all directions. At the surface, however, the force acts only sideways or downwards. This uneven force is called surface tension and pulls the water's surface into a tight skin that tiny organisms can stand on. To them it feels like a trampoline.

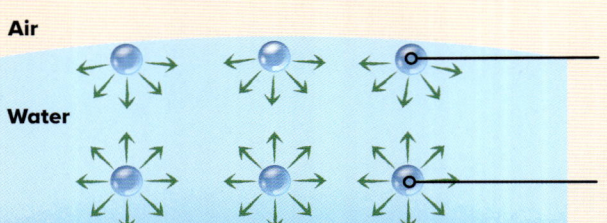

At the surface, water molecules are pulled sideways and downwards.

Below the surface, molecules are pulled in all directions.

Walking on water

Some insects take advantage of the surface tension of water to hunt other insects that fall in and get trapped.

Pond skater
Water-repellent feet allow pond skaters to glide on the surface. They hunt by feeling the water for the vibrations of prey trapped in the surface.

Whirligig beetle
These predatory beetles keep their main body and front legs above the water, but their middle and hind legs submerged for swimming.

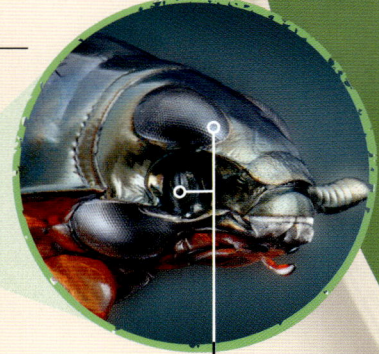

Whirligig beetles have two pairs of eyes – a pair to see in air and a pair to see underwater.

How it works: snowflakes

Every snowflake starts around a microscopic speck, such as a dust particle or pollen grain, inside a cloud. Water vapour freezes into ice on the speck, forming ice crystals, which grow as the snowflake spins around in the frozen air. The exact shape in which the crystals grow depends on the humidity and temperature the snowflake encounters as it travels. No two snowflakes share the same path to the ground, so each one is a unique record of its journey.

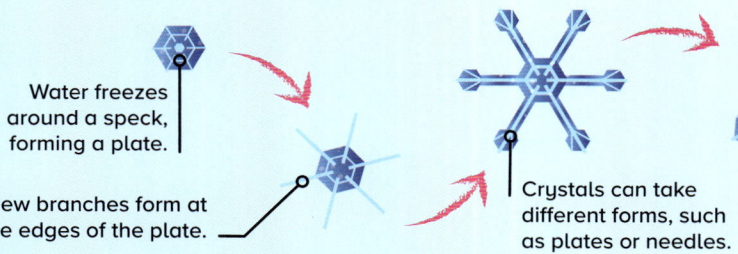

Water freezes around a speck, forming a plate.

New branches form at the edges of the plate.

Crystals can take different forms, such as plates or needles.

Each branch is identical as each has the same path.

Complex patterns can form when humidity is high.

Snowflake

Snowflakes are ice crystals that form high in the clouds. They look like fluffy white crumbs to the naked eye, but up close each has a beautiful pattern, as seen in this light microscope image. Each snowflake is unique, shaped by the temperature and humidity in the air as it tumbles to the ground.

Frost

Frost is a covering of ice crystals that appears on surfaces on cold nights when the temperature falls below zero. Like snowflakes, it can form beautiful patterns and shapes.

Ground frost occurs when the cold ground chills the air above it to below 0°C (32°F).

Hoar frost forms when water vapour in the air freezes directly onto cold surfaces.

Fern frost has feathery, fernlike patterns, and forms on cold glass windows.

Rime ice appears when cold fog droplets are blown onto surfaces and instantly freeze.

Natural antifreeze

Since water expands as it freezes, winter can be lethal to animals in freezing conditions. If ice formed in their blood, it could burst their blood vessels. Many fish and insects, and some frogs — such as the wood frog (below) — have evolved a natural antifreeze that prevents ice forming in their bodies.

All snowflakes have a hexagonal shape because of the way water molecules line up when they freeze.

Snowflakes start out as flat shapes called plates.

Snowflakes with broad arms that form a star shape are called stellar plates.

Beautiful dendrite (treelike) snowflakes, with feathery branches, form in very cold, moist conditions.

The **largest** snowflake ever recorded was discovered on a ranch in **Montana**, USA, in **1887**. It was **38 cm** (15 in) wide and **20 cm** (8 in) thick.

Being buffeted by ocean waves smooths any rough edges on the grains, so they look like precious gemstones.

This wheel-like particle may be a tiny piece of the hard skeleton of a coral.

This branching structure is a spicule, which forms part of the skeleton of a sea sponge.

Olivine is a dense, green-coloured mineral. It forms in huge amounts deep inside Earth.

Sand

To the naked eye, sand may not look very exciting, but seen up close it is surprisingly beautiful. Sand forms from rocks or seashells that break down into tiny grains over thousands of years due to the action of waves and the weather. When magnified hundreds of times, it is possible to see the extraordinary variety of different things that make up just a tiny pinch of sand.

A **bucket** can hold **hundreds of millions** of sand grains.

Sand makers

The fine white sand found on many tropical beaches is mostly made of parrotfish poo. Parrotfish nibble at hard corals, to get to algae growing on and inside them. Extra teeth located inside their throats grind up the hard coral, which they excrete (poo) as white sand.

Black sand

Islands that were formed by volcanic eruptions, such as Iceland, Hawaii, and the Canary Islands, often have striking black sand beaches. Over millions of years, dark volcanic rock is ground down by the sea to form black sand.

Industrial uses

Sand is one of the most used materials on the planet. Each year, billions of tonnes are used to make bricks and concrete, and millions more to make glass. The chemical element silicon is extracted from sand to make microchips used in electronic devices.

A microchip is built on a thin wafer of silicon.

Giant rocks

When grains of sand are squashed together over a long period of time, they stick together to form a rock called sandstone. Uluru in Australia is a massive red sandstone formation, the size of 30 football pitches.

How it works: Chalk

Most of the chalk we see formed in warm, shallow seas between 140 and 65 million years ago. The billions of coccolithophore skeletons that piled up on the ocean floor created a thick layer of sediment called lime mud. Over time, geological processes removed the water from the lime mud and compacted it, slowly turning it into rock. Later, sea levels dropped, revealing the white chalk cliffs we see today.

Chalk

The chalk we use for writing and drawing is a soft, crumbly rock made from the skeletons of billions of tiny organisms. These microscopic algae, called coccolithophores, build protective shells made from the mineral calcium carbonate. When they die, the tiny shells sink to the sea floor and over millions of years turn into chalk. Close up, these shells are among the most beautiful found in nature.

The plates separate when the coccolithophore dies.

Many types of ancient starfish have been found in chalk.

Carbon catchers

The main cause of climate change is the release of carbon dioxide (CO_2) into the atmosphere from human activities. Coccolithophores can help to counter this. They reduce CO_2 levels in the sea and atmosphere by taking in CO_2 for photosynthesis. The carbon is then locked away in their shells, which sink to the sea floor.

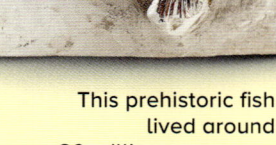

This prehistoric fish lived around 80 million years ago.

Chalk fossils

The tiny skeletons of coccolithophores that make up chalk are themselves microfossils. But chalk is a great material for finding the fossilized remains of bigger animals. It is hard enough to preserve the animal's shape but soft enough for the fossils to be easily excavated. Most fossils found in chalk are of small sea creatures such as ammonites, sea sponges, and echinoids (sea urchins). Very rarely the remains of larger animals, even dinosaurs, have been preserved.

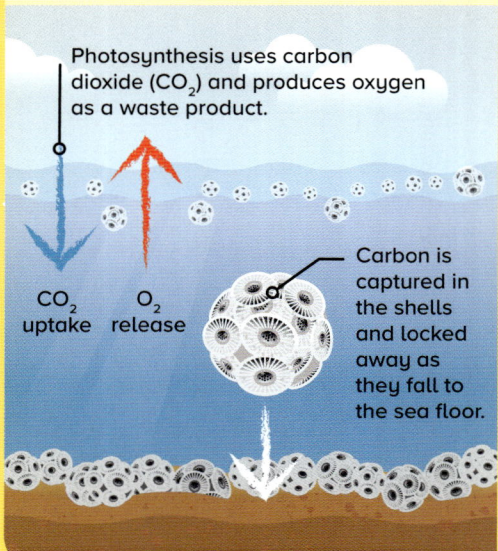

Photosynthesis uses carbon dioxide (CO_2) and produces oxygen as a waste product.

CO_2 uptake
O_2 release

Carbon is captured in the shells and locked away as they fall to the sea floor.

How it works: Bacteria

Bacteria have been around for over 3.5 billion years – since long before dinosaurs – and are the most plentiful organisms on Earth. One reason for their amazing success is that they can reproduce at incredible speed. Bacteria make copies of themselves by a simple process of cell division: a single cell divides to form two identical cells. In the right conditions a single bacterium can divide to form more than 100 in just over two hours.

Each cell divides in two, allowing a colony (group) to grow very quickly.

Bacteria

These microscopic organisms live almost everywhere, including in soil and water and on skin. A mobile phone may look clean to the naked eye, but as this microscope image shows, a touch-screen is home to a whole community of bacteria. In fact, a mobile phone carries 10 times more bacteria than a toilet seat.

Heat-loving bacteria turn the pool rainbow colours as they photosynthesize.

Extremophiles

Extremophiles are organisms, including bacteria, able to live in extreme environments where other life isn't possible, such as hot springs, deserts, and ice sheets. Bacteria have even survived a trip to outer space. A kind of bacterium called *Chloroflexus* thrives in the volcanic hot springs of Yellowstone National Park, USA, where water temperatures reach 87°C (188°F).

These *Micrococcus* bacteria live in soil, dust, and on skin.

This electron microscope image shows bacteria magnified 16,500 times.

Skin bacteria

Every one of us is teeming with bacteria. In fact, our bodies have more bacterial cells than human cells. This image shows the millions of bacteria and other microorganisms grown in a lab from a human handprint. Around 1,000 bacteria species live on human skin, feeding on dead skin cells and sweat. Most of them are harmless but some bacteria can cause infection if they enter a cut and multiply.

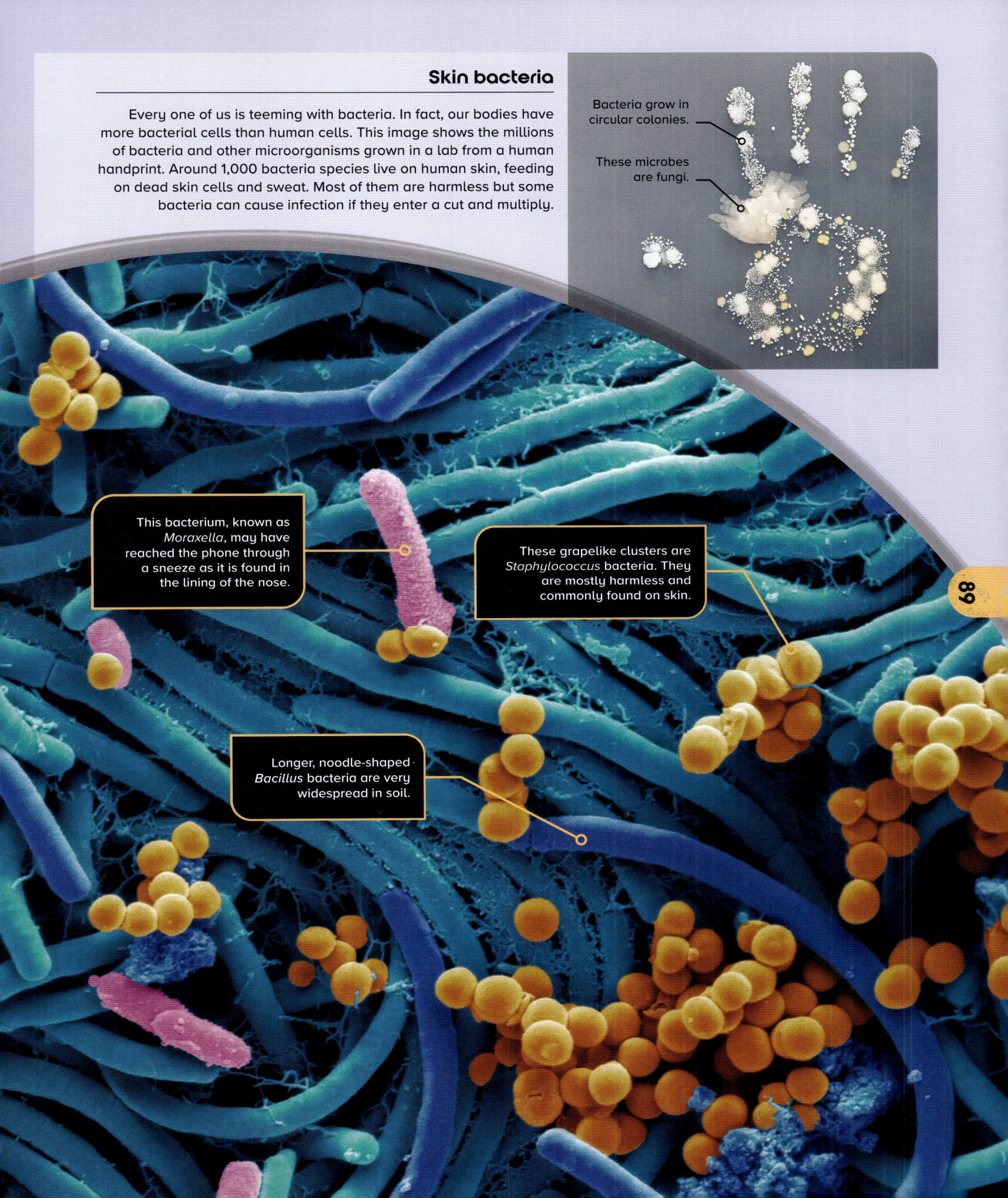

Bacteria grow in circular colonies.

These microbes are fungi.

This bacterium, known as *Moraxella*, may have reached the phone through a sneeze as it is found in the lining of the nose.

These grapelike clusters are *Staphylococcus* bacteria. They are mostly harmless and commonly found on skin.

Longer, noodle-shaped *Bacillus* bacteria are very widespread in soil.

Algae

Algae are simple, plant-like organisms found in oceans and freshwater. They are crucial to the ecosystem, both as a food for aquatic life and because they produce around half the oxygen we breathe. This alga is called spirogyra and looks like green slime if you pick it up. However, when it's magnified 900 times you can see the beautiful inner workings of its long green threads.

Glow in the dark

Some species of alga produce light through a chemical process called bioluminescence. It is triggered by movement or threats, and can be confusing to predators. Wave action can be enough to cause algae to glow.

Algae attack

When algae grow quickly in huge numbers, it is known as an algal bloom. This happens when nutrients are washed off land into waterways. The algae feed off the nutrients and grow so thickly that they block sunlight. The algae beneath die and decay, which makes oxygen levels fall. This creates "dead zones" in the water where plants and animals struggle to survive.

How it works: Spirogyra

Spirogyra is a green alga found in freshwater, formed of threads a single cell wide. At the centre of each cell is a nucleus, the cell's control centre, which is held in place by tiny threads of a jelly-like substance called cytoplasm. Winding around inside the cell is the green, spiral-shaped chloroplast. It captures energy from the Sun, which the cell uses to make food. This process produces oxygen, which is then released into the air.

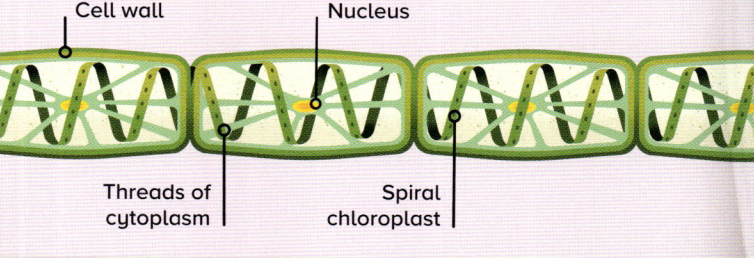

Cell wall · Nucleus · Threads of cytoplasm · Spiral chloroplast

There are at least 72,500 species of algae.

Giant kelp

While many algae are microscopic, some can grow to be enormous. The biggest species of alga is giant kelp, which can grow by 60 cm (2 ft) a day and reach 60 m (195 ft) long. Vast underwater forests of kelp provide a sheltered habitat for all sorts of animals, including these sea lions.

Spirogyra grows in slimy mats that float on the water surface.

The long strands of spirogyra are made up of single cells joined end to end.

Spirogyra gets its name from the spiral-shaped chloroplasts that wind through each cell. These trap the Sun's energy.

A rigid cell wall, made of a substance called cellulose, surrounds each cell and provides structure and protection.

Spirogyra can grow to several centimetres in length but are usually no more than 0.006 cm (0.002 in) wide.

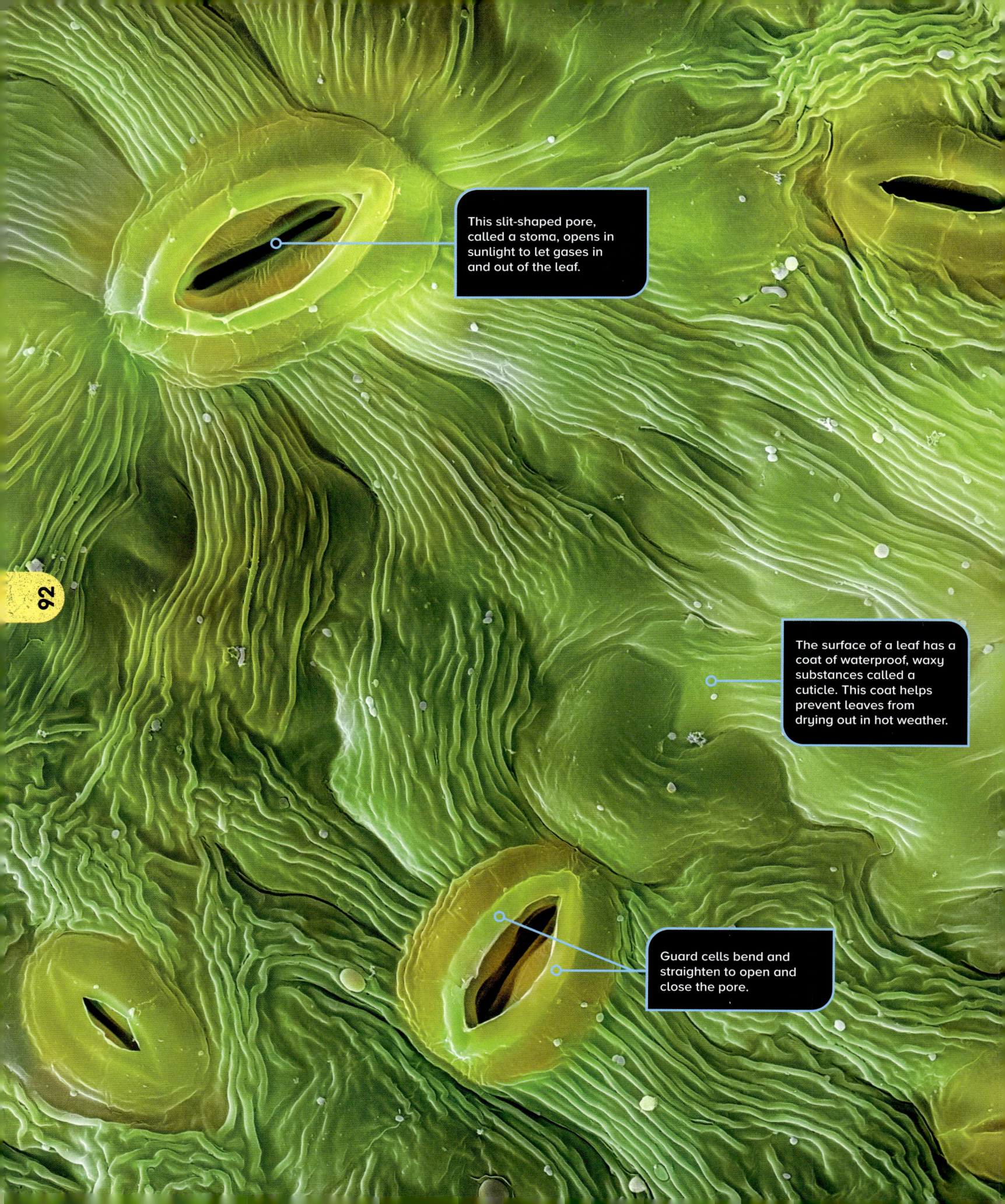

This slit-shaped pore, called a stoma, opens in sunlight to let gases in and out of the leaf.

The surface of a leaf has a coat of waterproof, waxy substances called a cuticle. This coat helps prevent leaves from drying out in hot weather.

Guard cells bend and straighten to open and close the pore.

Leaf

Leaves are the factories of plants. They use sunlight, water, and carbon dioxide gas to make sugars for energy and growth, and they release oxygen gas as a waste product. Gases enter and exit plants through tiny pores, called stomata, seen here magnified 3,000 times in a microscope image of an ash tree leaf.

The leaves of the **raffia palm** can grow to **25 m (82 ft)** long.

Stomata are mostly on the underside of leaves, shaded from direct sunlight.

How it works: Stoma

Most stomata open in the daytime when leaves need carbon dioxide gas and sunlight to make sugars. Two guard cells, at the entrance of the stoma, fill with water in sunlight. This makes them stiff and curved, and an opening forms that lets gases in and out of the leaf. Once it's dark, the guard cells lose water and sag, closing the stoma.

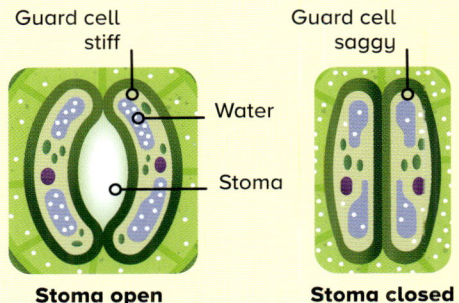

Inside a leaf

The upper and lower surfaces of a leaf are made of flat cells, called epidermal cells. A waxy coat known as a cuticle covers both surfaces. Inside the leaf are column-shaped palisade cells, which carry out most of a plant's photosynthesis (in tiny, green structures called chloroplasts). Below the palisade cells are spongy cells with spaces around them for gases to circulate.

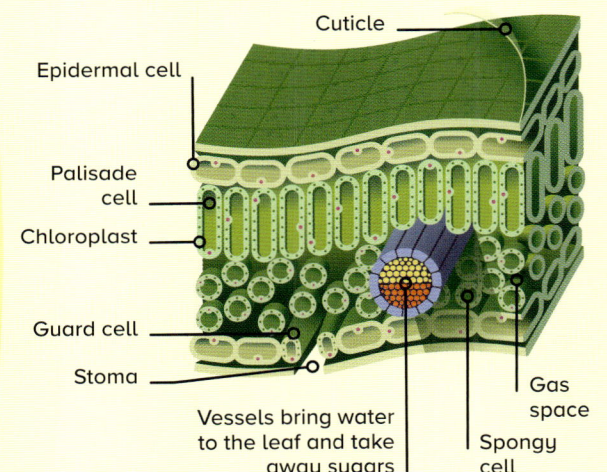

Photosynthesis

Plants capture energy in sunlight and use it to make sugars by a process called photosynthesis. Carbon dioxide gas and water are the raw ingredients needed to make the sugars. Carbon dioxide is in the air and enters plants through their stomata. Water comes from the soil and is absorbed by roots. Oxygen gas is a waste product of photosynthesis. All the oxygen breathed by animals, including humans, entered the atmosphere by photosynthesis.

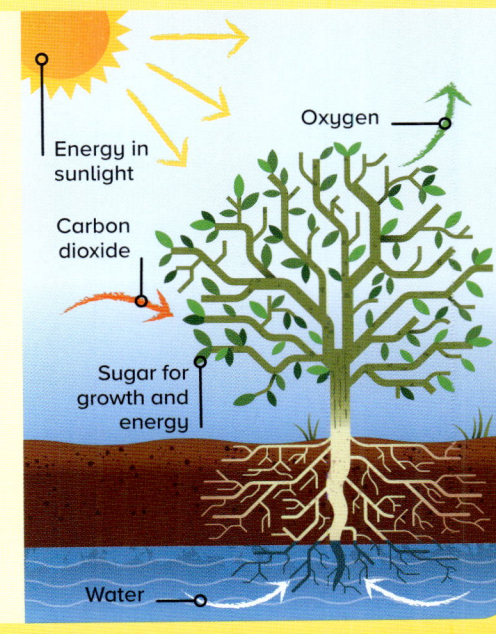

Leaf surface

Leaves appear wide and flat. That shape helps them catch more sunlight as they harness the Sun's energy to make food. But up close, leaves are not flat at all. They are covered in tiny structures called trichomes. These serve different purposes and make leaf surfaces hairy, rough, or even spiked.

Peppermint leaf

This leaf is covered in oil-producing trichomes. Up close, these oil glands appear as dark, shiny blobs. The oil gives the leaves a strong smell and flavour that puts off plant-eating animals. This doesn't work on us — we even use the taste of mint in sweets and ice cream.

These hair-shaped trichomes don't make oil. They protect the leaf from cold weather and insects.

Lotus leaf

The leaves of lotus plants float on water and need to be water-resistant so they don't get soggy. The top surface of each leaf has millions of microscopic bumps coated in a layer of waterproof wax. Together, the bumps and wax stop water spreading out and force it to form spherical droplets. These roll off the leaf easily, leaving it dry.

The water-repelling surface helps keep the leaf clean as water droplets wash away dirt.

Olive leaf

Olive trees grow in places that have long, hot summers. Their leaves are covered in flattened trichomes, shaped a bit like umbrellas. They overlap to create an extra waterproofing layer that stops the leaf's water evaporating away in the heat. The covering also protects the leaf from harmful ultraviolet rays in sunlight.

Trichomes with this shape are described as being peltate, which means "like a shield".

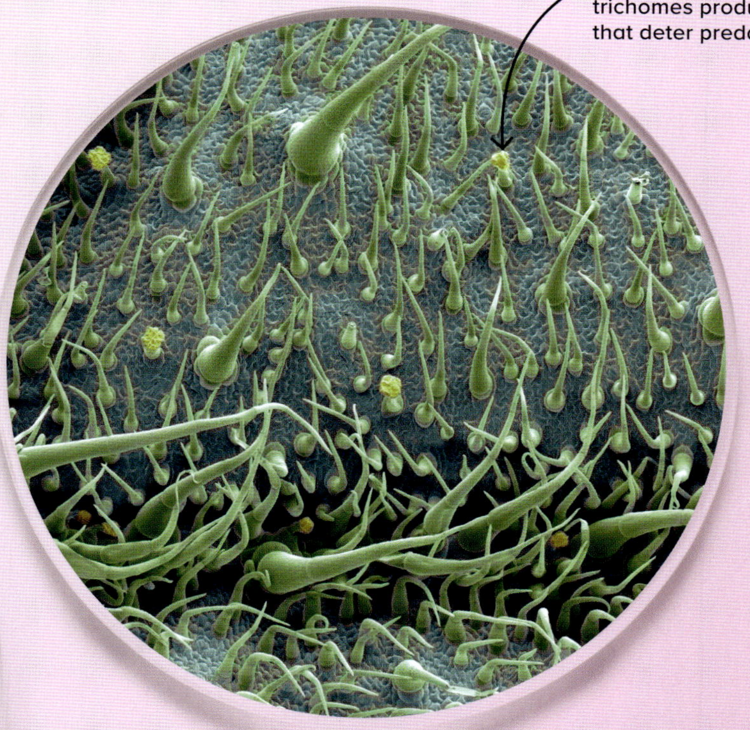

These short, stubby trichomes produce oils that deter predators.

Hibiscus leaf

There are many types of hibiscus plant, each producing beautiful trumpet-shaped flowers. The leaves have two kinds of defensive trichome. The chubby stumps produce an oily liquid that protects the leaf surface from rain and microorganisms. The tall spiky ones prickle the mouths of leaf eaters and contain chemicals that create a burning sensation.

Spiky trichome

Oil-making trichome

Tomato leaf

The trichomes on tomato leaves form a forest of tiny spiky hairs that make it hard for leaf-eating insects to reach the surface. The hairs also trap a layer of damp air next to the leaf, which stops it drying out on hot days. Other trichomes produce a sticky liquid that glues to insects, making it even harder for them to get through.

The stem is covered in tiny stinging and non-stinging hairs, which are also found on the leaves.

Stinging, needlelike hairs contain a cocktail of venomous chemicals.

Shorter, more flexible hairs do not sting.

How it works: Stinging nettle

At the end of each hollow, needle-shaped stinging hair is a fragile glasslike bulb. When a person or animal brushes up against the plant, these bulbs snap off, each leaving behind an incredibly sharp tip that pierces the skin and delivers a dose of irritating chemicals. The sting is sharp enough to stop most hungry animals who try to eat these nettles from ever trying again.

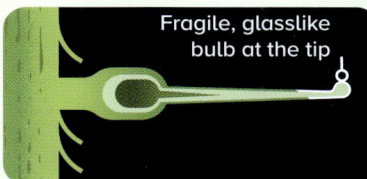

1. Stinger
Main shaft of the stinger hair has an outer wall hardened with minerals.

2. Bulb breaks
The tip snaps off when something or someone brushes past the stinger.

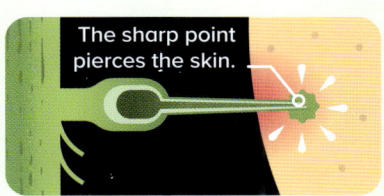

3. Piercing the skin
The sharp point penetrates the skin and releases irritating chemicals.

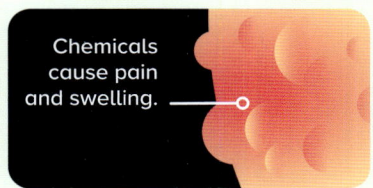

4. Venom delivered
The chemicals cause a sharp, painful sting and skin swelling.

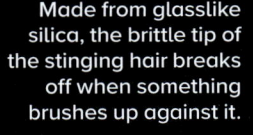

Made from glasslike silica, the brittle tip of the stinging hair breaks off when something brushes up against it.

Stinging nettle

Compared to a prickly cactus, a leafy nettle might look relatively harmless. But when you get up close, the two don't look so different. The tiny hairs covering the surfaces of this plant are actually needlelike weapons that can deliver a sharp surprise.

Dark green, heart-shaped leaves grow in opposite pairs.

Food for caterpillars

Despite their sting, nettles make a great habitat for lots of different species of caterpillars and other insect larvae that are not troubled by the stinging hairs. Red admiral butterflies, found in Europe, Asia, and North America, lay a single egg on nettle leaves. The caterpillar then feasts on the leaves from the day it hatches to when it gets ready to transform into a butterfly.

Female lays single egg on leaf

Egg attached to tip of nettle leaf

Hatched caterpillar feeds on nettle leaves

Pollen

Bees get covered in pollen when they visit flowers for nectar.

Flowering plants reproduce by making sex cells. The female cells stay inside the flowers, but male cells make the perilous journey from plant to plant. They do so in grains of pollen, which float on air or hitch a ride on animals. Seen here magnified over 1,000 times, pollen grains are as beautiful and varied as the flowers they come from.

Pollen carriers

Some flowers are pollinated by animals. Such flowers attract their pollinators with colourful petals, scents, or a sugary drink called nectar. The pollen grains often have spiky shapes or a sticky surface to help them cling to the visitor. Animal pollination helps plants because the pollen has a good chance of reaching its target: another flower of the right species.

*Some plants can make a **billion** pollen grains in **one** summer.*

A pollen tube has begun to emerge in the middle of this tulip pollen grain.

Pollination

If a pollen grain lands on the female part of just the right kind of flower, it sprouts like a miniature plant and a tube grows deep into the flower. This is called pollination. The pollen tube releases a male sex cell, which combines with a female cell (an egg cell) inside the flower so that a seed can form.

Pollen grows into the flower's ovary, where seeds develop.

Blowing in the wind

Some plants rely on wind to transport pollen. Wind is less reliable than animals, so these plants make billions of pollen grains to ensure a few will land by chance on another flower. Wind-borne pollen grains are tiny and float in the air like dust. In spring and summer, the air we breathe carries so much pollen that it gives some people a runny nose and sore eyes. This allergy to pollen is called hay fever.

Solving murders

Every species of plant makes a unique kind of pollen. This sometimes helps forensic scientists solve murders. By identifying the pollen on shoes or clothes, they can tell if a suspect visited a crime scene. Pollen buried for centuries in tombs, glaciers, or soil can also tell us about the plants and climate of the past.

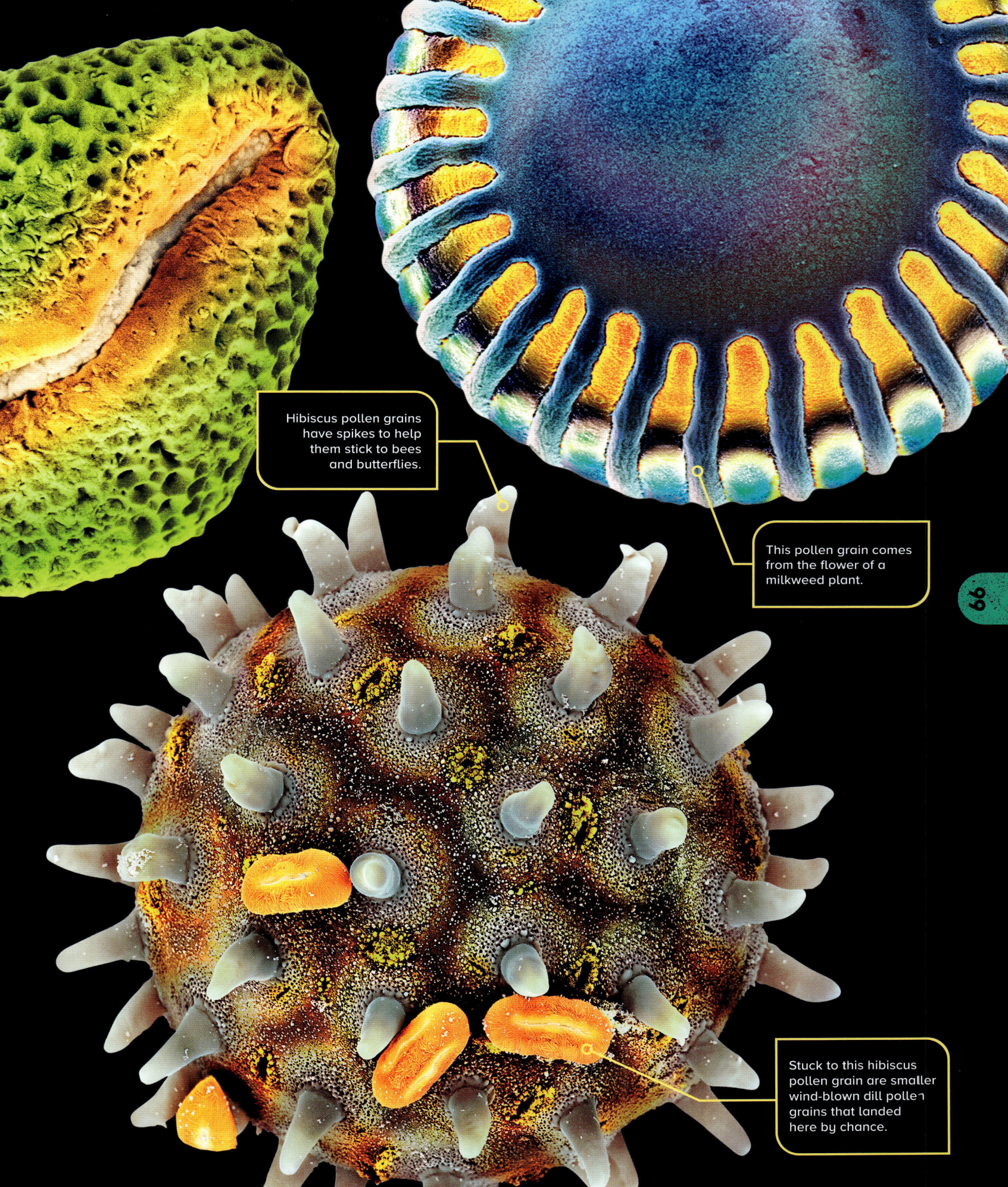

How it works: Germination

A seed germinates (grows into a plant) when the soil is warm and moist, and has plenty of air. First, it takes in water and swells, splitting open its protective coat. A root grows downwards from the seed, taking in water and nutrients from the soil. A shoot then sprouts, growing upwards towards the light.

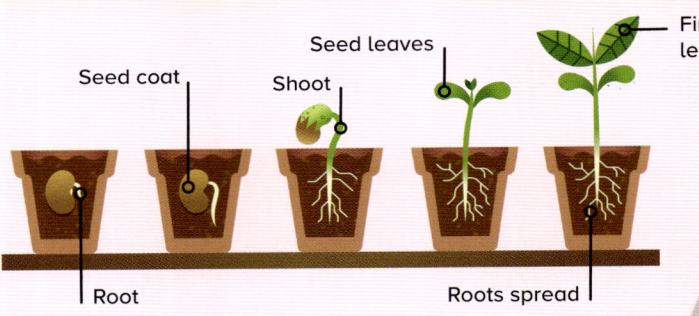

Seed

A seed contains everything needed for a new plant to start growing. The smallest seeds are microscopic – the largest are the size of a bowling ball. This electron microscope image shows a sesame seed (the kind of seed found on a burger bun) magnified 100 times.

A sesame seed's coat is covered in tiny bobbles.

Seed dispersal

Plants have a variety of ways to make sure their seeds get scattered far and wide. This is called seed dispersal.

Wind
Dandelion seeds are carried by the wind – sometimes for miles – using their own parachutes.

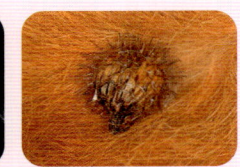

Animals
Burdock burrs have hooks that stick to animal fur, taking the seeds to new locations.

Water
Coconut palms grow on beaches. Their fruits are washed into the sea by waves and float off to new lands.

Explosions
Like sesame, Himalayan balsam has capsules that explode, flinging out seeds in all directions.

Sandbox tree seeds **explode** from their **pods** with enough **power** to fire them **40 m** (130 ft) away.

Inside a seed

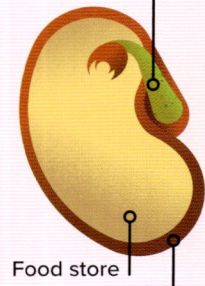

The part of a seed that grows into a new plant is called the embryo. It has a food store that it uses until it has grown leaves, when it will be able to make its own food by a process called photosynthesis. A seed coat covers and protects the seed.

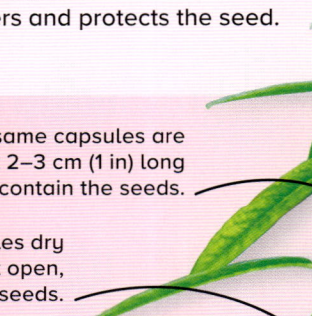

Sesame capsules are about 2–3 cm (1 in) long and contain the seeds.

When the capsules dry out, they burst open, scattering their seeds.

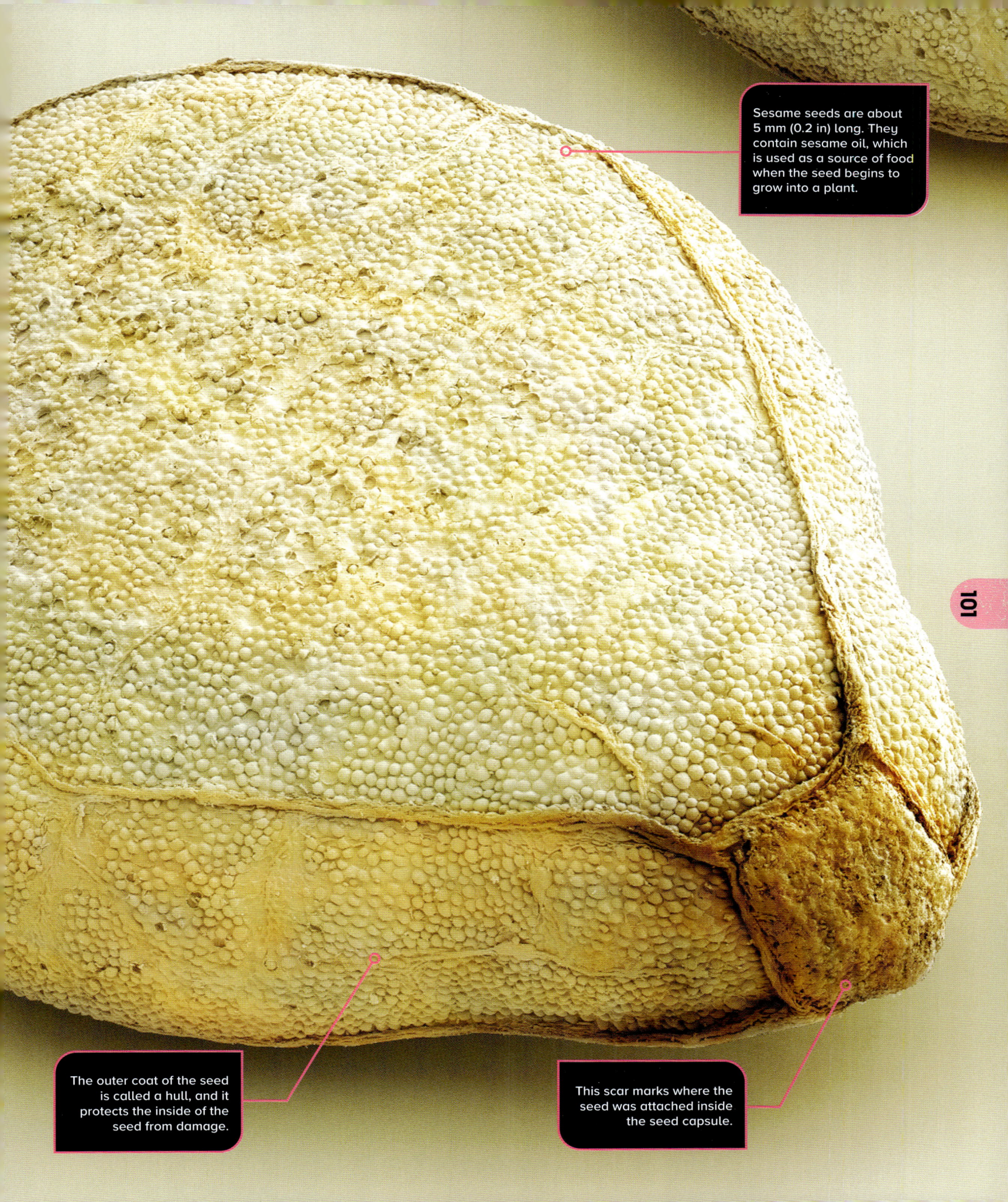

Sesame seeds are about 5 mm (0.2 in) long. They contain sesame oil, which is used as a source of food when the seed begins to grow into a plant.

The outer coat of the seed is called a hull, and it protects the inside of the seed from damage.

This scar marks where the seed was attached inside the seed capsule.

Daisy

How many flowers are in this picture? The answer might surprise you because it's not one — it's more than a hundred! This is a daisy, a type of flower known as a composite flower. Although it looks like a single bloom, it is in fact hundreds of tiny flowers tightly packed together. A sunflower, which works the same way, has more than a thousand tiny flowers in it.

How it works: Daisy

The tiny flowers that form a daisy are called florets, and there are two types. Ray florets are petal-like structures, which form a ring. They help to attract pollinators, such as bees, to the centre, where the disc florets are found. Disc florets make nectar, pollen, and seeds.

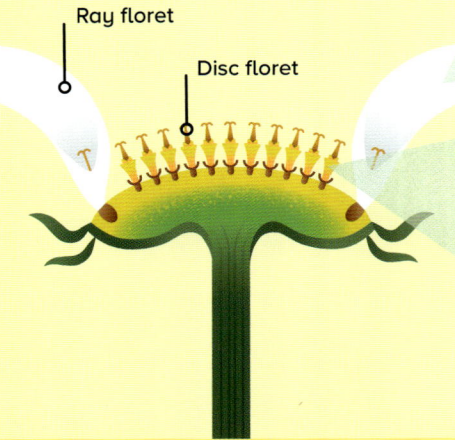

Ray floret
Disc floret

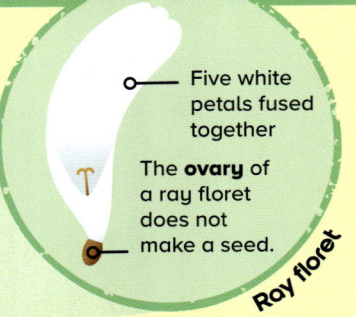

Five white petals fused together

The **ovary** of a ray floret does not make a seed.

Ray floret

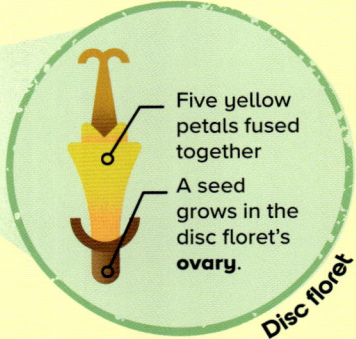

Five yellow petals fused together

A seed grows in the disc floret's **ovary**.

Disc floret

Nectar guides

A daisy's ray florets help bees to find the disc florets at its centre, where there is nectar and pollen. The florets reflect ultraviolet (UV) light, which bees can see, but we can't.

We see a yellow flower with a dark brown centre.

Visible light

Bees see a circular pattern that guides them to the flower's centre.

UV light

Daisies are **edible** and high in **vitamin C**.

Daisies unfurl their petals during the day and close them at night.

This disc floret hasn't opened yet.

This yellow stalk is an anther – the male part of a floret. It makes pollen.

Each disc floret has five small yellow petals fused into a tube.

Suprising fruits

The word "fruit" makes us think of sweet and juicy things like apples and grapes. However, to a scientist, a fruit is the part of a plant that contains seeds and that develops from the heart of a flower after pollination. Squashes, cucumbers, and many other vegetables are also fruits in the scientific sense, even though they aren't sweet.

Hazelnuts
Some fruits are hard and dry, such as hazelnuts, walnuts, and acorns.

Butternut squash
Although we call squashes vegetables, they are really fruits as they have seeds on the inside.

Olives
They may taste bitter and oily, but olives are fruits containing a single large seed called a stone.

Strawberry

A strawberry is not actually a fruit, scientifically speaking. It's the tiny golden pips, called achenes, dotting its surface that are the real fruit. Each pip — seen here magnified 150 times — contains a single seed. The seeds are spread in the droppings of animals that eat the strawberry, and then grow into new strawberry plants.

The world's heaviest strawberry weighed 322 g (11.35 oz) – as much as a grapefruit.

Strawberries have about 200 pips (achenes) on their surface.

How it works: Strawberry

When a strawberry flower is pollinated by bees or other insects, it starts to develop tiny fruits (achenes) around a central, conical part of the flower called a receptacle. The receptacle swells and ripens into a bright red fleshy "fruit", as the achenes mature on its surface. Strawberry plants live for several years and produce about 1 kg (2.2 lb) of strawberries each year.

1. Strawberry plant flowers
2. Receptacle of flower swells
3. Pale green achenes spread out as receptacle gets bigger
4. Flesh of strawberry turns red
5. Ripe, red strawberry with golden achenes

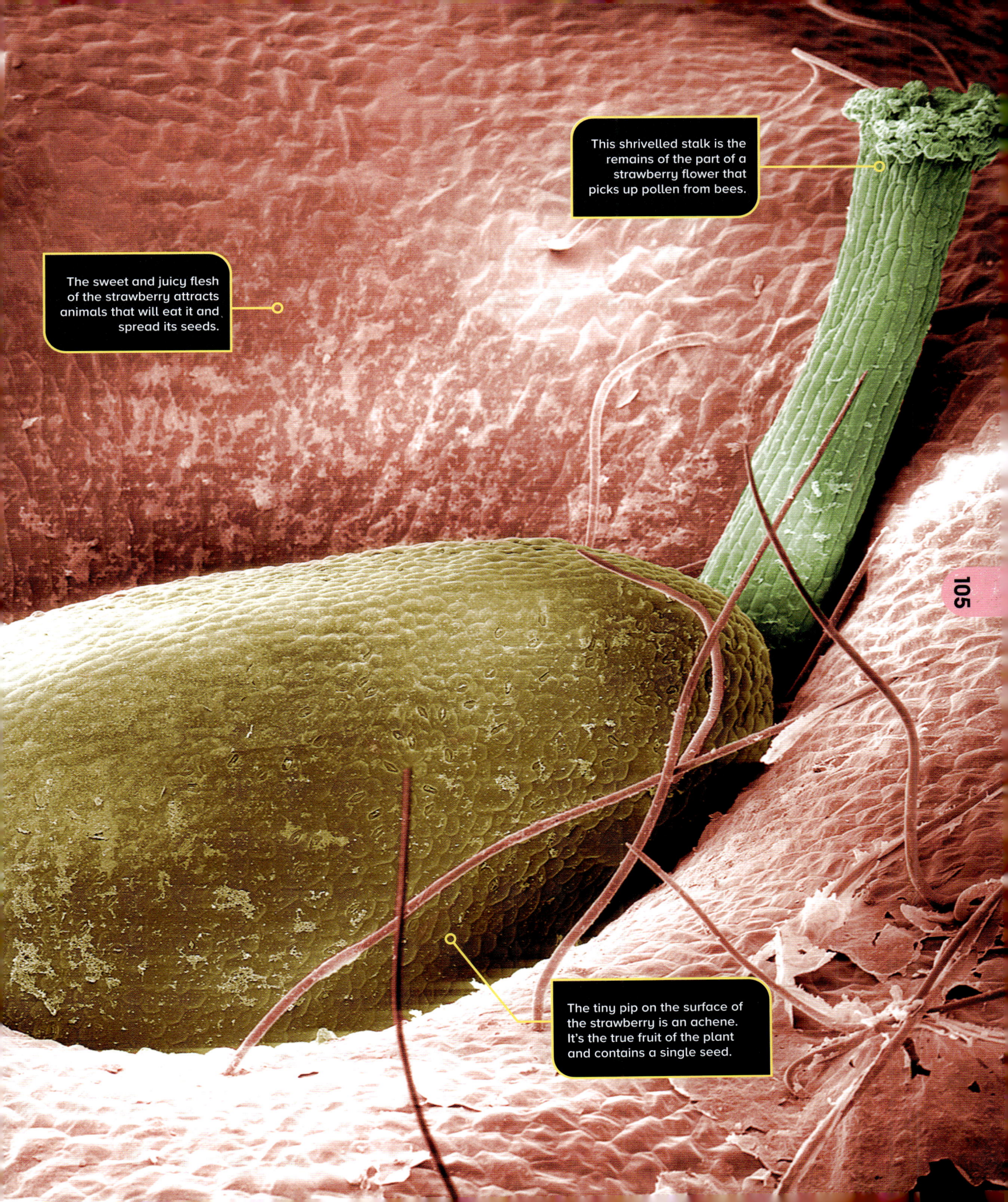

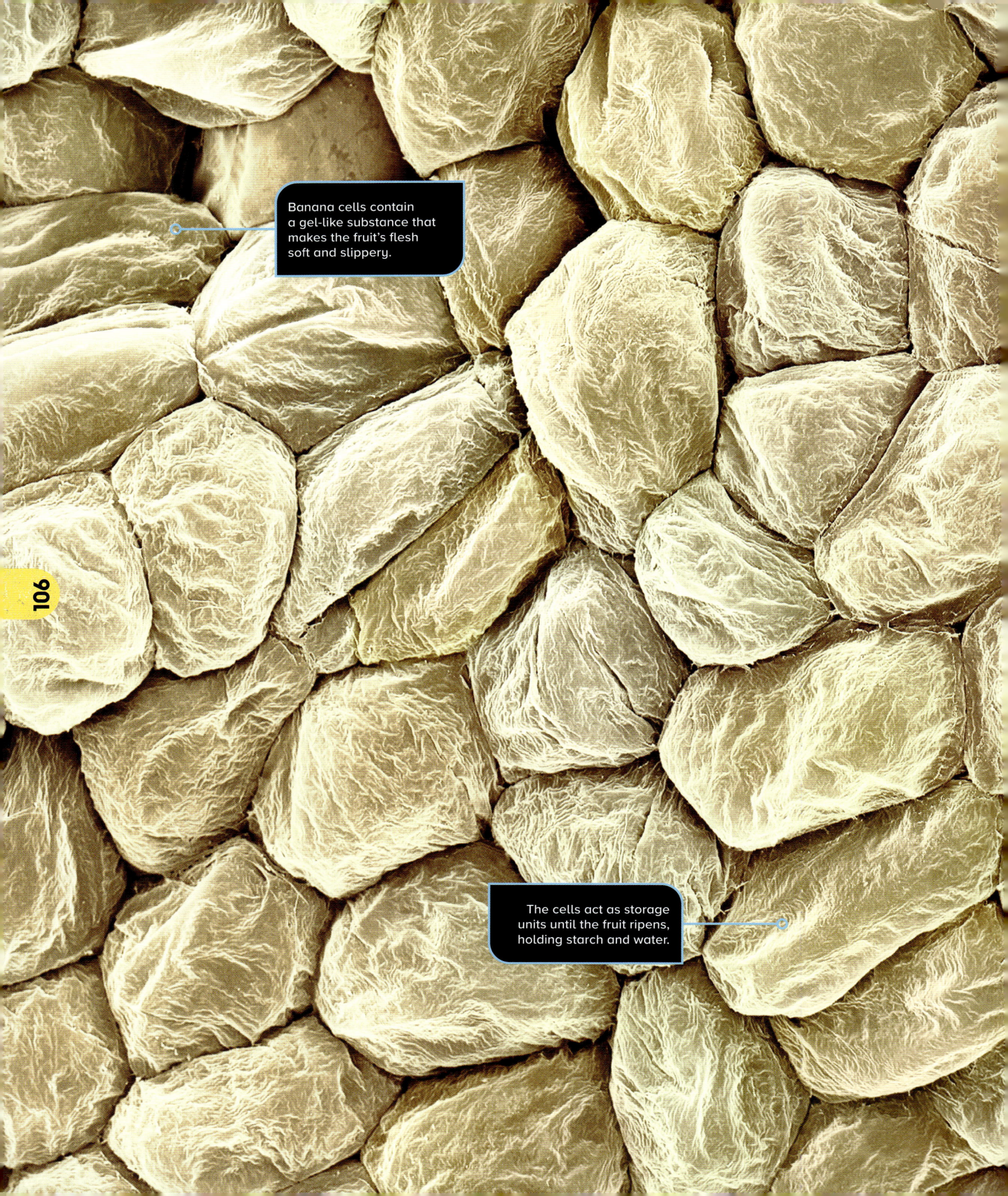

Banana

Bananas are the world's favourite fruit, with more than 100 billion eaten globally every year. Named from the Arabic for "finger", they have been a part of the human diet for thousands of years. This electron microscope image shows the surface of a banana magnified 1,000 times, revealing individual cells.

Banana ripening

Bananas, like all fruit, go through chemical changes during ripening that make them change colour and turn sweet. Unripe bananas contain lots of bitter-tasting starch. When it's time to ripen, the banana releases a gas called ethylene. The gas triggers chemical changes within the banana that break the starch down into sweet-tasting sugars and soften the flesh.

Unripe bananas have green skin and can photosynthesize.

Ethylene triggers the ripening process, causing the green skin to turn yellow.

Brown speckles appear, indicating that the fruit is ready to eat.

Overripe bananas have brown skin and mushy flesh.

Ethylene from a banana can make other fruits **ripen faster** if they are put together.

Banana clones

Wild bananas have seeds, but the kinds we grow for eating are seedless. So how do the plants reproduce? Bananas grow small shoots (pups) that are genetically identical to the parent plant. These are cut off and replanted. This is a quick way to grow new plants, but because they are all clones one disease could wipe them all out.

1. Starting life
A young banana plant grows.

2. New pup
The plant grows a pup at the base.

3. Separation
The pup is cut off and planted.

4. Clones
Each new plant is genetically identical.

Why are bananas curved?

Bananas get their distinctive shape because they grow upwards towards the light. Young banana fruits are straight at first, growing in bunches that point down towards the ground. As they mature, they bend, ensuring that each banana gets the maximum possible exposure to sunlight.

How it works: Venus flytrap

The Venus flytrap only snaps shut for a worthy meal, such as an ant or a fly. It waits for repeated movement before trapping its prey, avoiding false triggers like falling leaves. Once closed, the movements of the prey activate more sensory hairs. This prompts the plant to release digestive liquids that begin to break down the prey, releasing much-needed nutrients.

1. Attracting prey
Insects are attracted to the trap by its fruity scent.

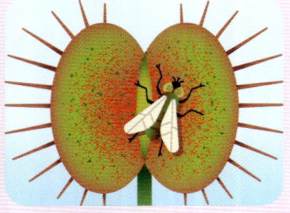

2. Triggering the trap
If the fly touches two or more hairs, the trap shuts.

3. Juices flow
The prey panics, triggering the flow of digestive juices.

4. Break down
The juices, made by special cells in the leaf, dissolve the insect's body.

Keeping pollinators safe

Carnivorous plants face a challenge – they need insects not just for food but also to pollinate their flowers so that they can make seeds. The Venus flytrap solves this problem by growing its flowers high above its traps. Attracted by sweet scents, pollinators like bees and beetles safely visit the flowers – avoiding the deadly traps below.

Venus flytrap

In the nutrient-poor bogs of the United States, one plant has turned predator to survive. The Venus flytrap has special leaves that form a deadly trap. They close in a tenth of a second when trigger hairs, shown here magnified 120 times, are touched by prey.

Flowers provide nectar to attract pollinators.

Stems raise the flowers up to 30 cm (12 in) above the traps.

Traps give off a fruity scent that attracts prey but not pollinators.

The teeth on the leaf edges interlock when the trap closes, forming a cage.

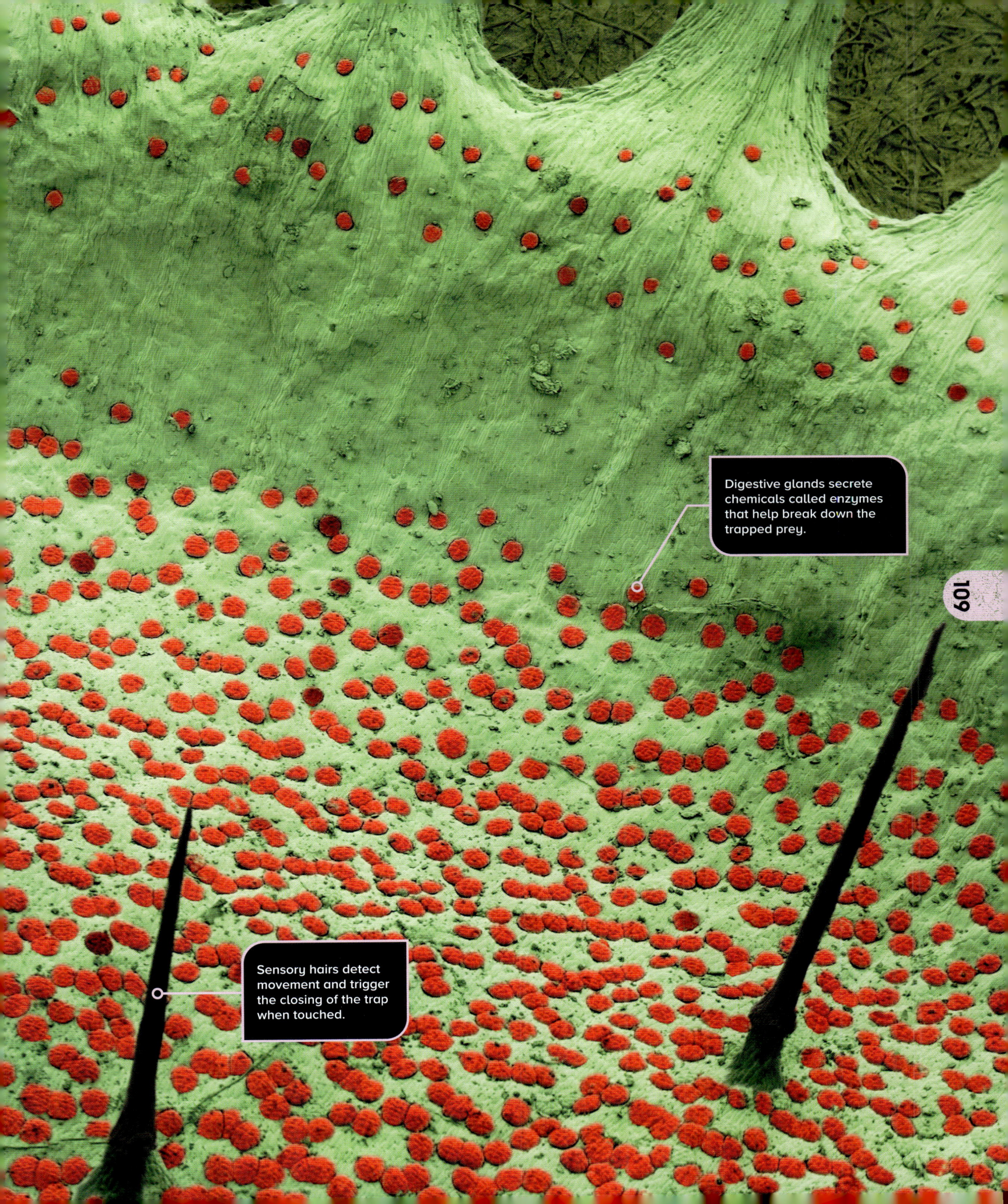

How it works: Tree trunk

A tree's trunk supports its structure but is also its transport system. Just beneath the bark is a layer of living cells called phloem. They transport sugars up and down the tree. Below this is a layer of pale wood called sapwood. This consists of xylem cells, which carry water up from the roots. Between the sapwood and phloem, new cells grow in the cambium layer, forming annual tree rings.

Over time, sapwood turns into strong heartwood at the tree's core.

- Phloem
- Sapwood
- Cambium
- Bark

Dark and light rings on a felled larch tree

Tree rings

Tree rings are like nature's diary. Each year, trees grow layers of cells in their trunk, which form rings — light rings in summer and narrow, darker ones in winter. This electron microscope image shows the rings inside a larch tree magnified 230 times. Such rings do not just reveal the tree's age but can also offer clues about weather conditions of the past.

Ancient trees

Dating trees by their rings is a field of science known as dendrochronology. By comparing the ring patterns of different trees in a region, scientists can also work out its past climate conditions. The oldest tree species that scientists have dated is the bristlecone pine of California, USA. Some of these trees are nearly 5,000 years old, making them a very useful record of climate history.

Prometheus, a **bristlecone pine** cut down in 1964, had **4,862** tree rings.

Comb jelly

These soft-bodied creatures are 95 per cent water, like jellyfish. Comb jellies are named for the eight rows of comb-like structures arranged along their bodies. These are formed of microscopic hairs called cilia. Comb jellies swim by paddling these cilia against the water, much like tiny oars. As they swim, they refract light, creating a rainbow of colours that can startle potential predators.

Long, sticky tentacles act like fishing lines to catch food.

Flounders swim upright as larvae.

Flounder larva

Many fish species start out life as planktonic larvae. One of the oddest is the flounder, which begins life looking symmetrical, like a normal fish. As it grows, one of its eyes slowly moves to the same side of the head as the other eye. At this point, the flounder settles on the bottom of the ocean, lying on one side with both eyes looking up so it can partly bury itself in sand for camouflage.

A water flea's body is encased in a transparent shell.

Water flea

Water fleas are small, transparent animals found in freshwater and are related to crabs, lobsters, and shrimp. These little creatures graze on algae and bacteria in lakes and rivers, helping control algae numbers and so keeping the water clear. They are themselves an important source of food for fish, insects, and amphibians.

The female water flea produces eggs that are clones of her, without mating.

Copepod

These long, spindly antennae are used for swimming.

Found in freshwater and saltwater all over the world, these tiny relatives of shrimps are the most abundant multi-celled organisms, making them a vital part of the marine ecosystem. Copepods feed on algae and remain as plankton their entire lives. This Calocalanus, like many copepods, has a single eye at the top of its head. It uses its beautiful, feather-like tail like a parachute to stop it sinking.

Plankton

A droplet of water from the sea, a pond, or even a puddle is teeming with all manner of microorganisms called plankton. Even a teaspoon of water will contain more than a million living things. Some are microscopic algae (phytoplankton) and others are tiny animals (zooplankton).

Ceratium is covered in protective armour.

The larva swims short distances using these little legs.

Hollow horns help the Ceratium float.

Crab larva

After hatching from its egg, a crab larva looks nothing like it will as an adult. This thin-shelled rock crab larva will spend weeks drifting as plankton. It will go through another planktonic stage, when it looks like a crab with a tail, before developing into a juvenile crab. It will then shed its shell repeatedly on its way to adulthood.

Dinoflagellate

Some plankton have characteristics of both plants and animals. This tiny Ceratium is a type of dinoflagellate, a single-celled plankton named for its flagella – two long tail-like structures that it uses to swim. Like all algae, it produces food through photosynthesis, but it can also capture and digest other plankton when needed.

Tardigrade

Meet the toughest critter on our planet! A fully grown tardigrade is only the size of a grain of sand but it can survive ice, drought, and temperatures as high as 150°C (302°F) or almost as low as −273°C (−460°F). Also called water bears or moss piglets, tardigrades are found around the world in moist environments or underwater.

Shrivelling up

When faced with dry or other harsh conditions, a tardigrade enters a kind of extreme hibernation. It sheds water and dries out. The result is a shrivelled husk called a tun. Tardigrades can survive in this inactive state without food and water for many years, only reviving when conditions improve.

Tardigrade Around 85% water

Tun Less than 1% water

Micro safari

Moist patches of moss and lichen contain vast numbers of tardigrades, along with a range of other microscopic animals.

Moss mites Usually less than a millimetre in size, these tiny relatives of spiders play dead when disturbed. When it's cold, their bodies make antifreeze chemicals.

Rotifers Rotifers have heads covered in cilia: tiny beating hairs that they use to waft food particles into their mouths and also for swimming.

Cilia

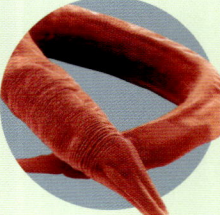

Nematodes These minuscule worms are among the most numerous animals on Earth – a teaspoon of soil contains thousands. They help recycle dead organic matter but can also cause diseases.

Space survivors

Astronauts have left tardigrades in space for ten days, without air, water, or protection from extreme temperatures or radiation, and found that two-thirds survived. Some live on the Moon, after a spacecraft carrying tardigrades crash-landed there in 2019.

Elegant eggs

There are more than 1,300 species of tardigrade. Many have spiky eggs to stick to things and stop them being washed away by rain. The eggs usually hatch after two weeks, but can survive much longer.

A patch of **moss** the size of a **bath towel** can contain as many as **2 million** tardigrades.

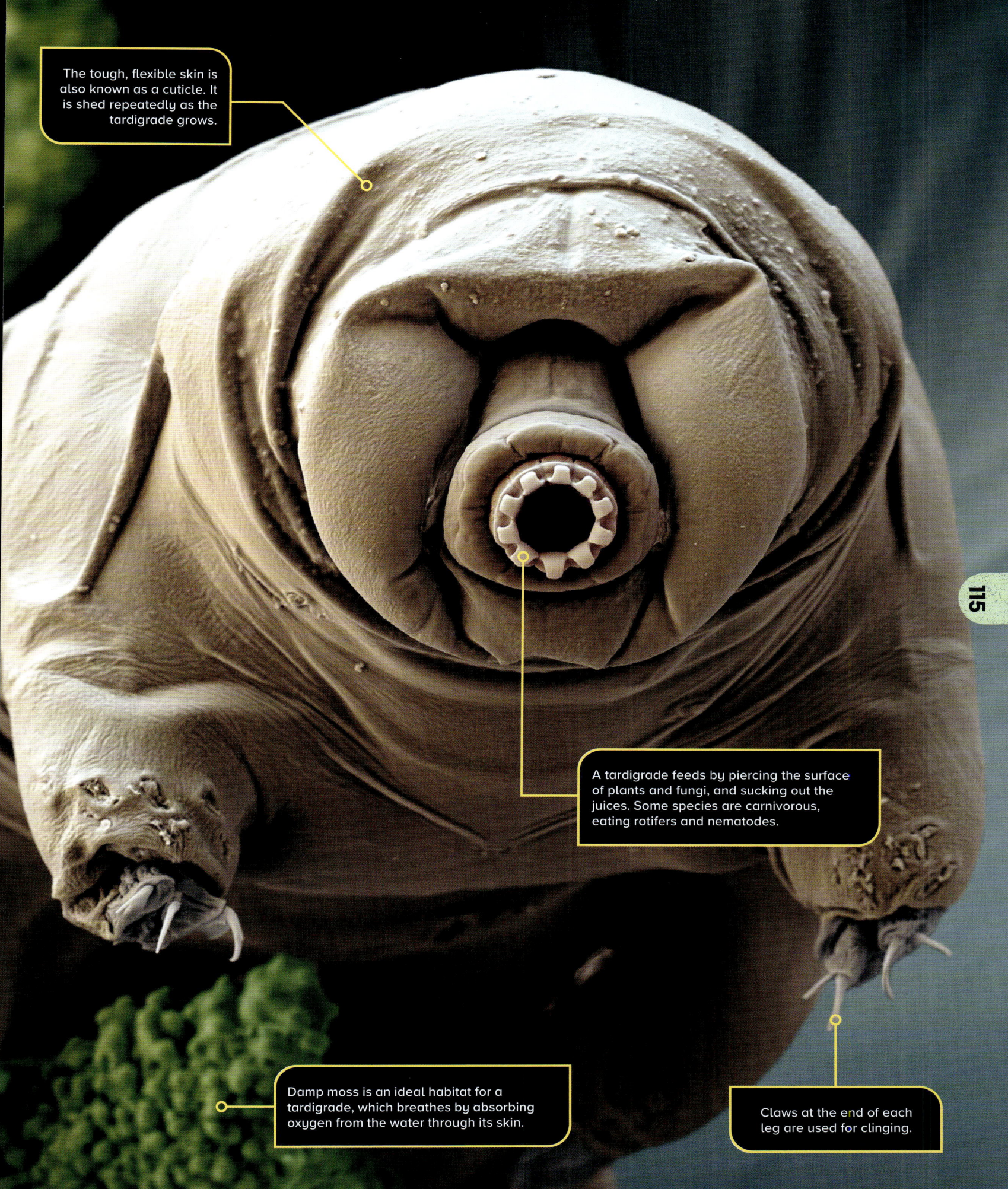

The tough, flexible skin is also known as a cuticle. It is shed repeatedly as the tardigrade grows.

A tardigrade feeds by piercing the surface of plants and fungi, and sucking out the juices. Some species are carnivorous, eating rotifers and nematodes.

Damp moss is an ideal habitat for a tardigrade, which breathes by absorbing oxygen from the water through its skin.

Claws at the end of each leg are used for clinging.

Although these indents look like little eyes, they are nasal pits, which the tadpole uses to detect smells in the water.

In its mouth, the tadpole grows a row of rasping teeth that it uses to eat plants and later small insects.

Adhesive glands secrete a sticky substance that lets tadpoles attach to surfaces.

Feathery gills hanging outside the body get oxygen from the water that flows past them.

How it works: Life cycle

Common frog tadpoles hatch and live in water. They have a long tail for swimming, and gills — like a fish — for breathing. Within weeks, their bodies begin to transform. Their legs grow, their tails shrink away, and gills are replaced by lungs, preparing the young frogs for life on land.

5. Frog
The frog lives mostly on land, but at 2–3 years old it returns to water to breed.

1. Frogspawn
Eggs in floating clumps just below the water's surface hatch within 3 weeks.

4. Froglet
The young frog absorbs its tail, moves onto land, and breathes using lungs 11–12 weeks after hatching.

3. Tadpole with legs
Hind legs grow first, then front legs.

2. Tadpole
The tadpole swims by flicking its tail sideways like a fish.

Tadpole

Have you ever seen a tadpole up close? By zooming in, it's possible to see its tiny eyes and mouth and the feathered gills it uses to breathe. It's just a few hours since this tadpole hatched from its jelly-covered egg. In several weeks, it will transform from a pond-dwelling tadpole into a land-living adult frog.

Only about 1 in 50 frog eggs make it to adulthood.

Hitching a ride

Unlike most other frogs, which lay their eggs in water, poison dart frogs in the rainforests of Central and South America lay their eggs on land. The parents carry the tadpoles on their back from moist egg-laying sites on the forest floor to small pools of rainwater that form in the overlapping leaves of bromeliads, plants that grow on tree branches.

Poison dart frog with tadpoles on its back

Common frog firing out its tongue to catch a fly

Changing diets

A frog's diet changes as it grows. A newly hatched tadpole's first meal is the jelly that surrounded it in its egg. It then moves on to eating algae and water plants, before feeding on water insects and sometimes other tadpoles. Adult frogs hunt small invertebrates, such as insects, worms, and slugs.

Earthworm

The world is full of worms — there could be more than a million different species. The one we see most is the earthworm. Scientists describe it as a segmented worm because its body is made of repeating parts (segments). This electron microscope view shows its eyeless head magnified 530 times.

What do earthworms eat?

Worms gulp down a third of their body weight in soil every day. Soil is made of clay and grains of sand mixed up with bacteria, fungi, and fragments of dead plants. Worms digest these food items in their long gut. Also known as a cast, worm poo often appears on the surface of the ground and looks a lot like soil.

A thickened segment called a saddle makes a slimy covering to protect eggs.

The last segment includes the worm's anus.

Pointed head

The world's largest earthworms live in Australia and reach 1 m (3 ft) long.

Worm relatives

Earthworms are related to other kinds of segmented worms that feed in different ways. Some of these relatives even have biting jaws with sharp teeth.

Sucker around leech's jaws attaches to skin

Medicinal leech
A leech's jaws bite and suck blood. Humans once widely used leeches to remove blood as a medical treatment. They are still used to improve blood flow after surgery.

Jaws extend out of mouth

Biting reef worm
This marine worm pokes its head up from the seabed. When it detects a nearby fish, its extended jaws snap shut and withdraw into the worm's head with its prey.

Soil health

Worms mix up the the layers of soil as they eat their way through it. Mixed-up soil has a better distribution of nutrients, making it better for plants. The tunnels left by worms also create spaces for air and water, which are vital for plant roots.

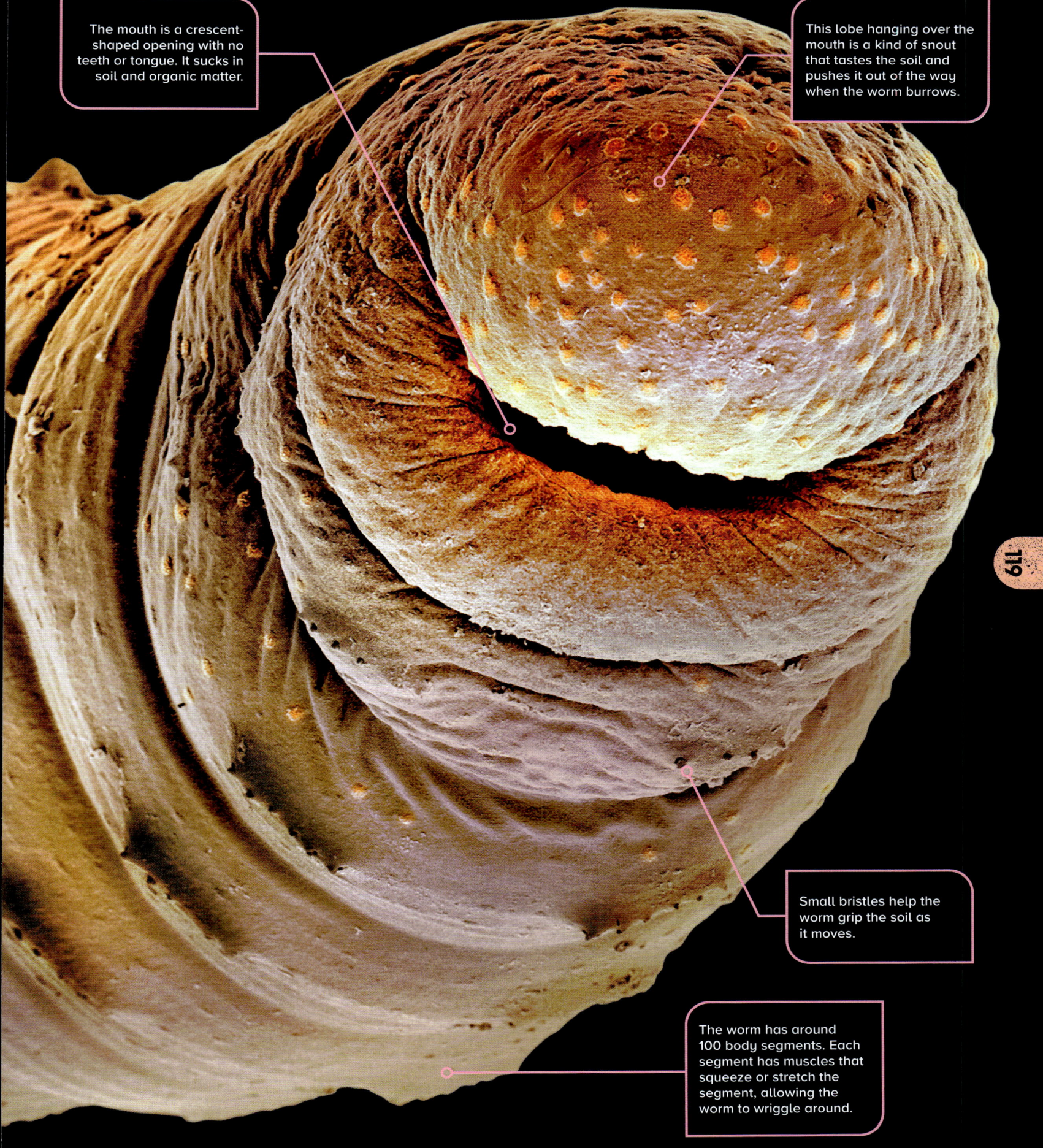

The tongue of the Roman snail has around 20,000 teeth. Each is less than a tenth of a millimetre long.

The denticles are arranged in overlapping rows with raised edges to trap food.

Snails' grinding tongues often leave feeding tracks on surfaces, such as this one on a garden fence.

Roman snail

How it works: Snail tongue

The radula works like a broom: its rough surface moves forwards and backwards, scraping against leaves and other plant material. The shredded food particles are hauled into the mouth to be swallowed.

Snail tongue

Did you know that a snail's tongue has teeth? The proper name for a snail tongue is a radula, which means "little scraper". At 2000x magnification you can see the tiny teeth, called denticles, which are used to scrape food from plants. Depending on the species, there are hundreds or even thousands of denticles on a snail's tongue.

The snail scrapes its radula against the surface of the plant.

Food particles

When not feeding, the snail pulls the radula back into this chamber.

Killer snail

Cone snails have a different kind of radula. It's shaped like a harpoon, with a pointed tip and a backward-pointing barb. They use it to stab prey and inject a deadly venom. The barb snags inside the victim, which is then pulled back along with the radula and swallowed. A thousand times more powerful than morphine, the venom is strong enough to kill a human.

Piercing tip

A barb prevents the prey slipping off.

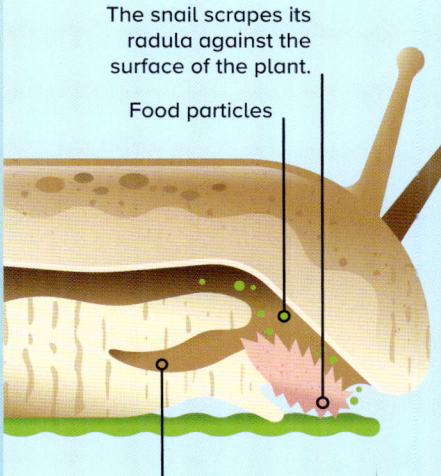

Superstrong teeth

Limpets are relatives of snails and live on rocky beaches. They have ultra-tough denticles strengthened by an iron-rich mineral for scraping food off rocks. Their teeth are so strong they can strip the surface of a rock.

Tracks left by limpets

How it works: Mosquito bite

When a female mosquito finds a host, she lands on its skin. She slides back the sheath of a long sucking tube called a proboscis. She uses the sharp tip of the proboscis to pierce the skin and pushes it in. She then pumps in saliva full of substances that stop the host's blood from clotting and numb any pain. She finds a blood vessel under the skin and slurps up the blood inside.

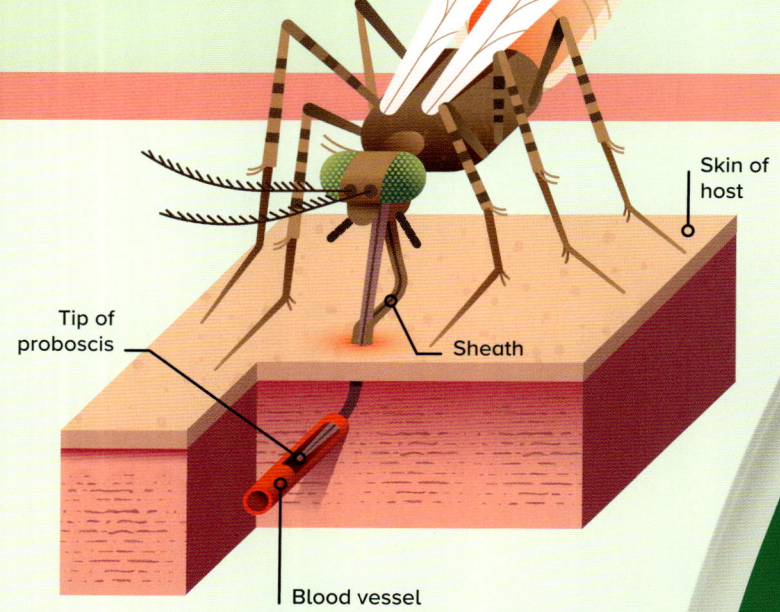

Mosquito

Mosquitoes have a bad reputation thanks to the itchy bites they inflict and their high-pitched buzzing. Only female adults bite, as they need the nutrients in blood to grow their eggs. To feed, they use their long, needlelike mouthparts to pierce their hosts' skin and suck up the blood.

A mosquito drinks just **one 10,000th** of a **teaspoon** of blood per bite.

Spreading disease

Malaria is a dangerous disease spread by mosquitoes that have been infected with parasites. As an infected mosquito feeds on blood, it can pass on the infection to its host. Once the host is infected, the parasites reproduce inside red blood cells. These cells swell in size and eventually burst, causing fever and releasing more parasites that infect other red blood cells. Malaria can be fatal without treatment.

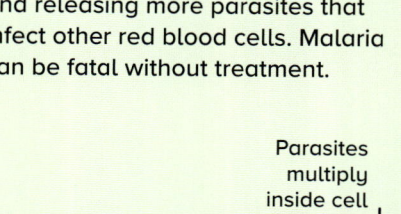

Normal blood cell is a flattened disc with a centre dip.

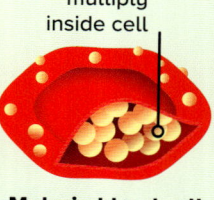

Malaria blood cell swells with parasites and bursts.

Immune response

The swelling, redness, and itching that follow a mosquito bite aren't caused by the wound itself. These symptoms appear because your immune system reacts to the mosquito's saliva. White blood cells detect it and release histamine, a chemical that causes irritation.

Nectar-feeding males

Male mosquitoes don't drink blood — they sip nectar and sap from plants. However, they still buzz around humans, probably because that's where female mosquitoes are. Hanging around nearby boosts their chances of finding a mate.

Mosquitoes find their next meal by using their antennae to detect carbon dioxide in a potential host's exhaled breath.

The sheath of the proboscis bends away as the tip of the proboscis pierces the skin.

The mosquito's abdomen swells with blood to several times its usual size.

While feeding, the mosquito gets rid of excess liquid – mostly water – from the blood, to make more space for nutrients.

The mosquito lifts its back leg while it feeds.

Spider silk

Spiders use their silk to capture food, protect eggs, build dens and even to fly. Spider silk is a marvellous material, studied by humans for its incredible strength and flexibility. Yet it starts as a thick goo, and up close you can see how it is squeezed out through tiny tubes on the spider's body.

How it works: Silk-making

Specialized silk glands in a spider's abdomen produce a thick liquid protein. The liquid is passed through ducts (tubes) that absorb water and turn it into fibres. The ducts lead to tiny structures at the end of the abdomen called spinnerets. Most species have three pairs of spinnerets, each containing dozens to hundreds of microscopic spigots. The fibres emerge through the spigots as solid threads of silk.

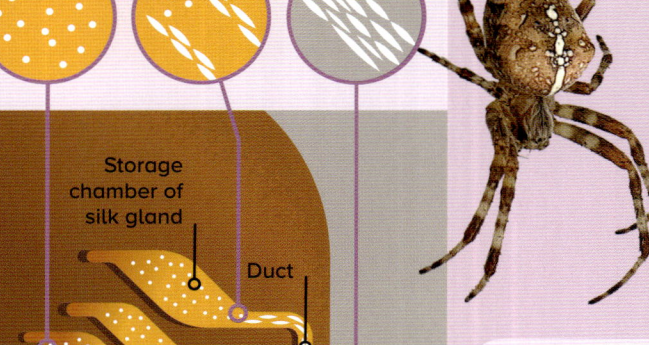

Droplets of silk protein — **Protein starts to solidify** — **Solid silk threads**

Storage chamber of silk gland — Duct — Spinneret

*Gram for gram, spider silk is **five** times **stronger** than **steel**.*

Each spigot has a valve that controls the position and thickness of the emerging thread. This works a bit like the nozzle of an icing bag.

Spiderlings

Baby spiders are called spiderlings and develop inside silk egg sacs made by their mother. The sacs may contain hundreds of eggs that all hatch at once. The babies then scurry away to find new homes. Some spiderlings disperse by floating in the air. They make a long strand of silk that catches the wind and carries them off for miles.

Baby spider on the move

Other silk producers

Other animals have also evolved the ability to produce silk or silky materials.

Female lacewings use silk to build stalks for their eggs. This prevents the first larvae to hatch from eating all the other eggs.

Webspinners spin silk from glands on their forelegs to build silk-lined tunnels and chambers. The insects use these as protection while they rummage about feeding on leaf litter, moss, bark, and lichen.

Silkworms are the larvae of the silk moth. The protective cocoons they weave around themselves contain up to 900 m (3,000 ft) of silk.

This electron microscope view shows a silk gland at 10,800x magnification.

The spigots can work independently, allowing the spider to combine threads and produce silk of different types and thicknesses.

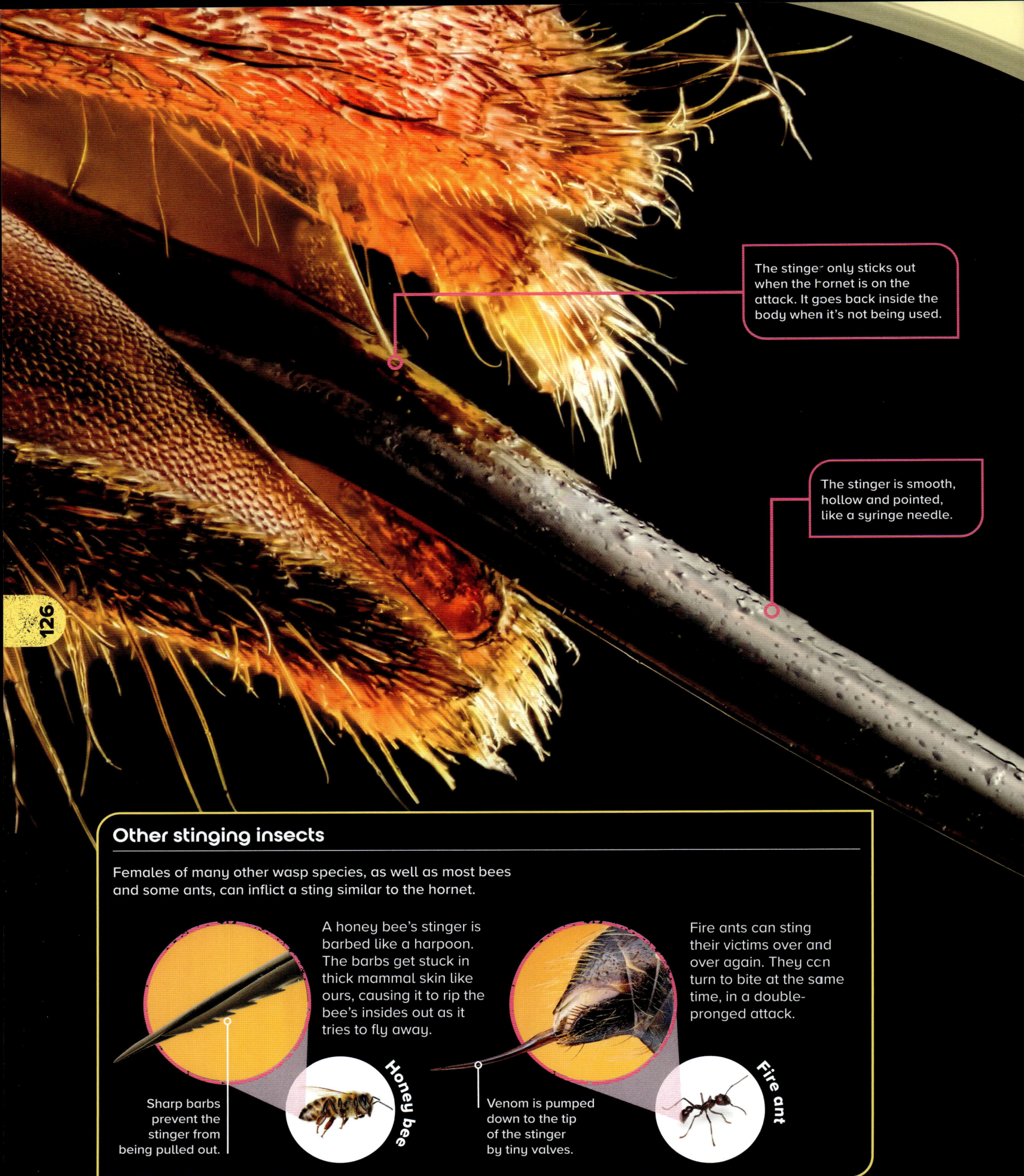

The stinger only sticks out when the hornet is on the attack. It goes back inside the body when it's not being used.

The stinger is smooth, hollow and pointed, like a syringe needle.

Other stinging insects

Females of many other wasp species, as well as most bees and some ants, can inflict a sting similar to the hornet.

A honey bee's stinger is barbed like a harpoon. The barbs get stuck in thick mammal skin like ours, causing it to rip the bee's insides out as it tries to fly away.

Sharp barbs prevent the stinger from being pulled out.

Honey bee

Fire ants can sting their victims over and over again. They can turn to bite at the same time, in a double-pronged attack.

Venom is pumped down to the tip of the stinger by tiny valves.

Fire ant

How it works: Hornet sting

The hornet makes venom in its venom gland and then stores it in a small sac called the venom reservoir. When it's time to sting, the reservoir's muscular walls contract to force venom out through the sharp, hollow stinger and into the victim's bloodstream.

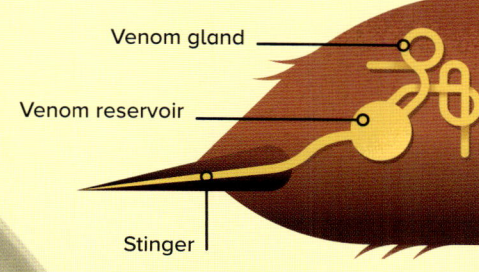

- Venom gland
- Venom reservoir
- Stinger

Why do stings sting?

The hornet's venom causes the victim's body to release histamine. This chemical makes nearby blood vessels expand, leaving the surrounding skin red, swollen, and itchy. Other substances in the venom trigger nearby nerve endings, producing a painful burning and stabbing sensation.

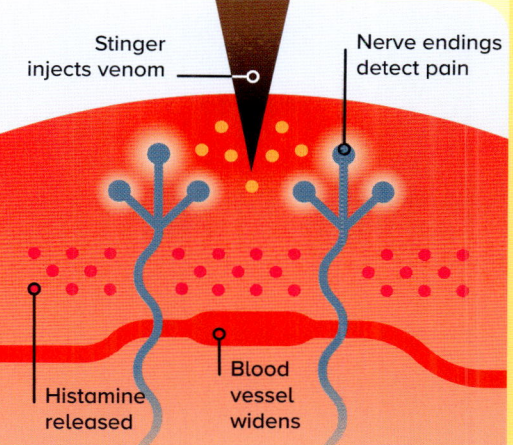

- Stinger injects venom
- Nerve endings detect pain
- Histamine released
- Blood vessel widens

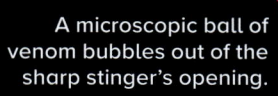

A female worker hornet can grow to around 2.5 cm (1 in), the same length as a paperclip.

A microscopic ball of venom bubbles out of the sharp stinger's opening.

Hornet sting

Hornets have a fearsome reputation for their stings, but they are actually less likely to use them than honeybees. They typically only sting to defend their nest or colony from intruders or potential predators. The venom, although just a painful pinch to a human, can be a deadly dose for an insect. Hornets can sting repeatedly if they need to.

How it works: Compound eye

The units in compound eyes are called ommatidia. Each has a clear hexagonal window on top and a round lens under it to focus light onto a cluster of light-detecting cells. When struck by light, these cells generate an electrical signal that rushes straight to the fly's tiny brain. The visual system is so quick that a fly can react to something it sees in a hundredth of a second.

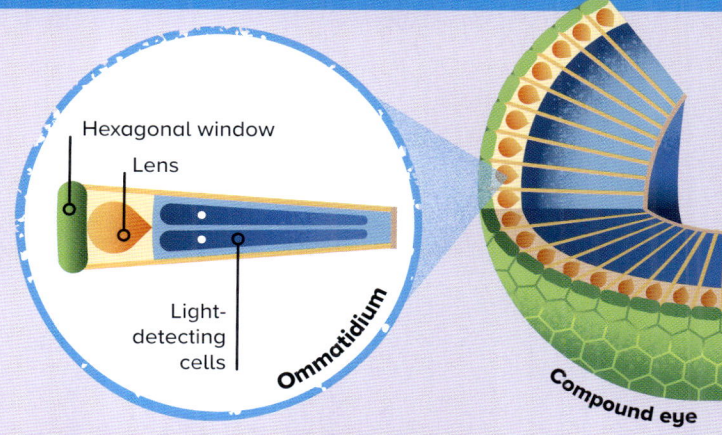

Compound eye

These wraparound eyes belong to a horsefly – a biting insect with a taste for blood. The compound eyes of insects are made of hundreds of small hexagonal units, each of which adds one pixel to the animal's vision. They have a much lower resolution than our eyes, but they are five times faster at detecting movement, giving insects lightning reactions.

Horseflies use piercing mouthparts to suck blood from horses and large animals.

A horsefly's wings beat 100 times a second.

How many ommatidia?

The more ommatidia in an eye, the higher the image resolution. Insects that live in the dark, like ants, have only a few hundred ommatidia. Skilful fliers such as dragonflies have as many as 28,000 per eye.

Shrimp super vision

Insects aren't the only animals with compound eyes. Crabs, shrimps, and lobsters have them too. The mantis shrimp has compound eyes on stalks and can swivel them separately to look in two directions at once. These eyes can also see colours invisible to us.

Early eyes

The first animals known to have compound eyes were the now-extinct trilobites, which lived in the sea 500 million years ago. The ommatidia in their eyes were made of solid crystal, making them super durable.

Butterfly scale

Wings and flight

Butterflies have four flexible wings – two triangular forewings and two fan-shaped hindwings. The two pairs beat together in flight but are not physically linked. On the upstroke, air between the wings is pushed out backwards in a jet as they meet, propelling the insect forwards. During the downstroke, the wings fling apart, drawing in air and boosting lift. This wing motion makes butterfly flight both graceful and surprisingly efficient.

Butterfly wings are covered in tiny, overlapping scales — like roof tiles. These scales protect the delicate wing membranes and streamline the wings for flight. Colours such as yellow and red come from chemicals in the scales, but shimmering blues and greens come from microscopic structures on their surface.

The upper surface of a blue morpho's wings are a shimmering blue.

With wings folded, the blue morpho blends into its background.

There may be as many as 600 scales in 1 sq mm (0.002 sq in) of a butterfly wing.

This vein gives the wing structural support and carries blood.

How it works: Scale colours

Some scales contain chemical compounds called pigments, which give the scale its colour by absorbing and reflecting certain wavelengths of light. Other scales have tiny ridges and layers that bend, scatter, and reflect light, creating colours even though there are no pigments present. This is called structural colour and can create iridescent (shimmering) colours that change when seen from different angles. Some butterfly scales have both pigments and structural colour.

Pigmentary colour

Black pigment absorbs all wavelengths and reflects none.

Red pigment reflects red wavelengths and absorbs all others.

Yellow pigment reflects yellow wavelengths and absorbs all others.

White pigment reflects all wavelengths and absorbs none.

Structural colour

Granules and ridges separate and bend light and can create iridescence.

Layered surfaces cause light to bounce around inside the layers, creating iridescence.

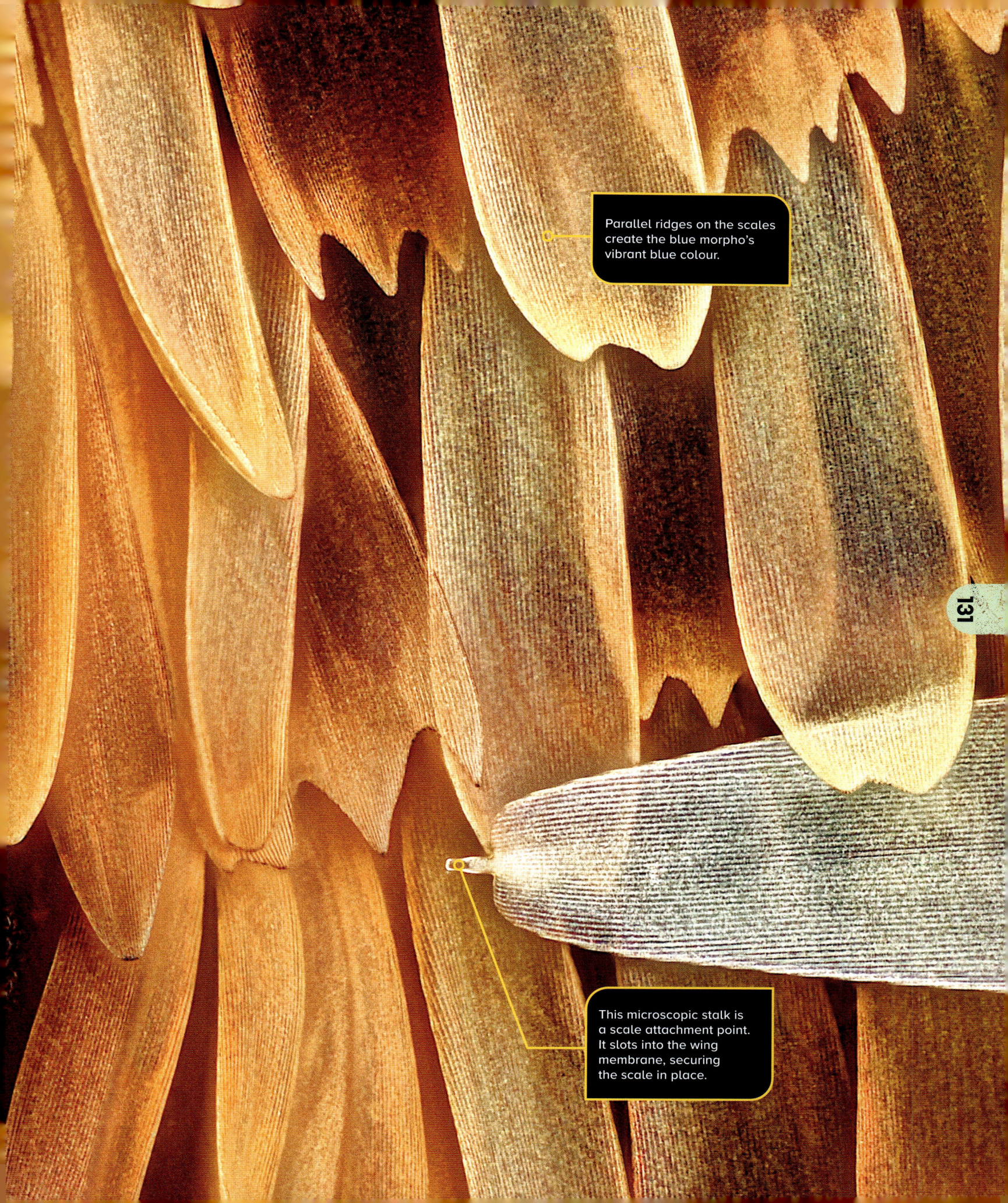

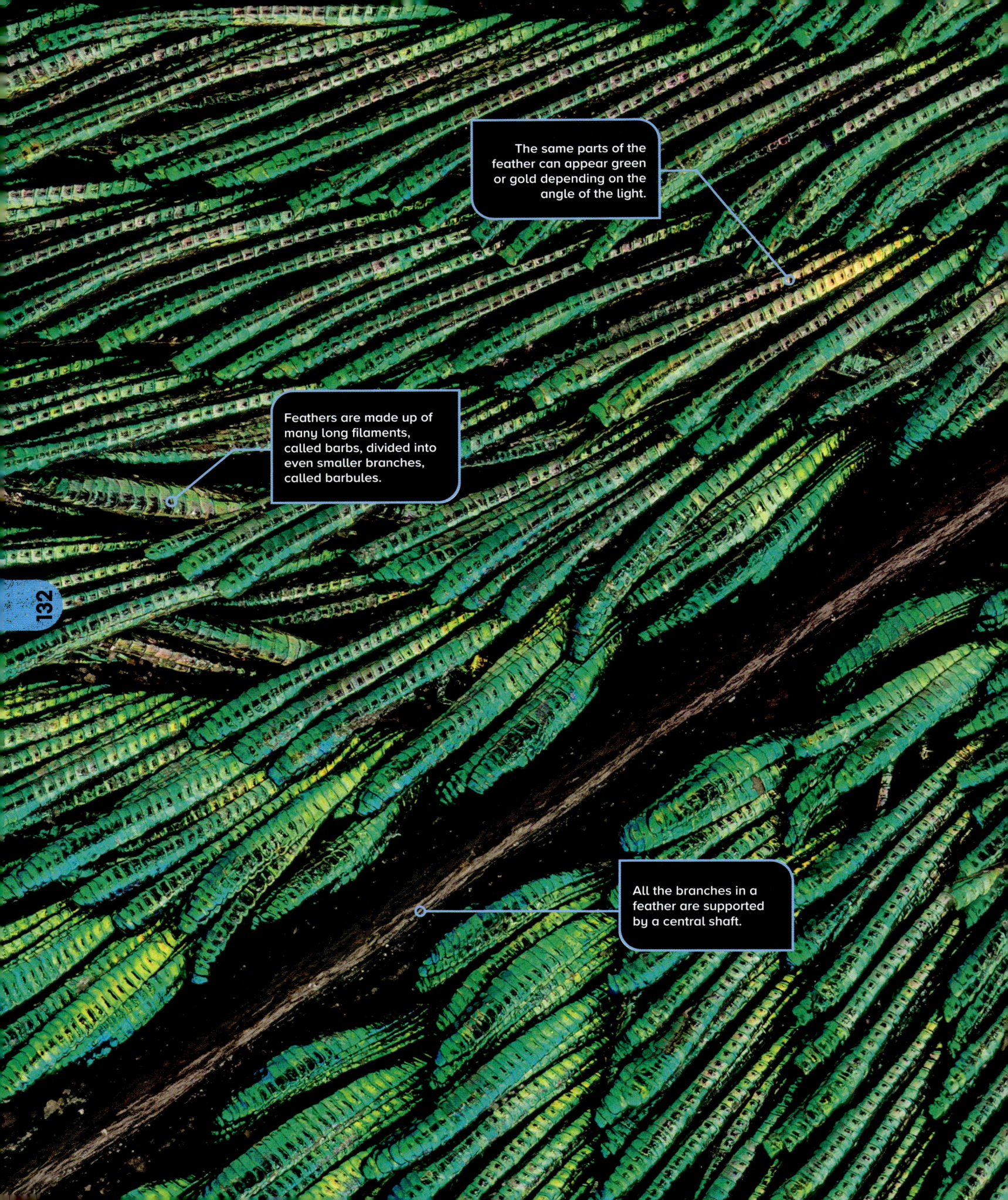

The same parts of the feather can appear green or gold depending on the angle of the light.

Feathers are made up of many long filaments, called barbs, divided into even smaller branches, called barbules.

All the branches in a feather are supported by a central shaft.

Fancy feathers

Peacocks fan their fancy feathers to attract females, known as peahens, in the breeding season. Afterwards, all the feathers are shed and the male must grow new ones the next year. The male's display is not just visual – he also vibrates the feathers to make a rattling sound that the female can sense through her head crest.

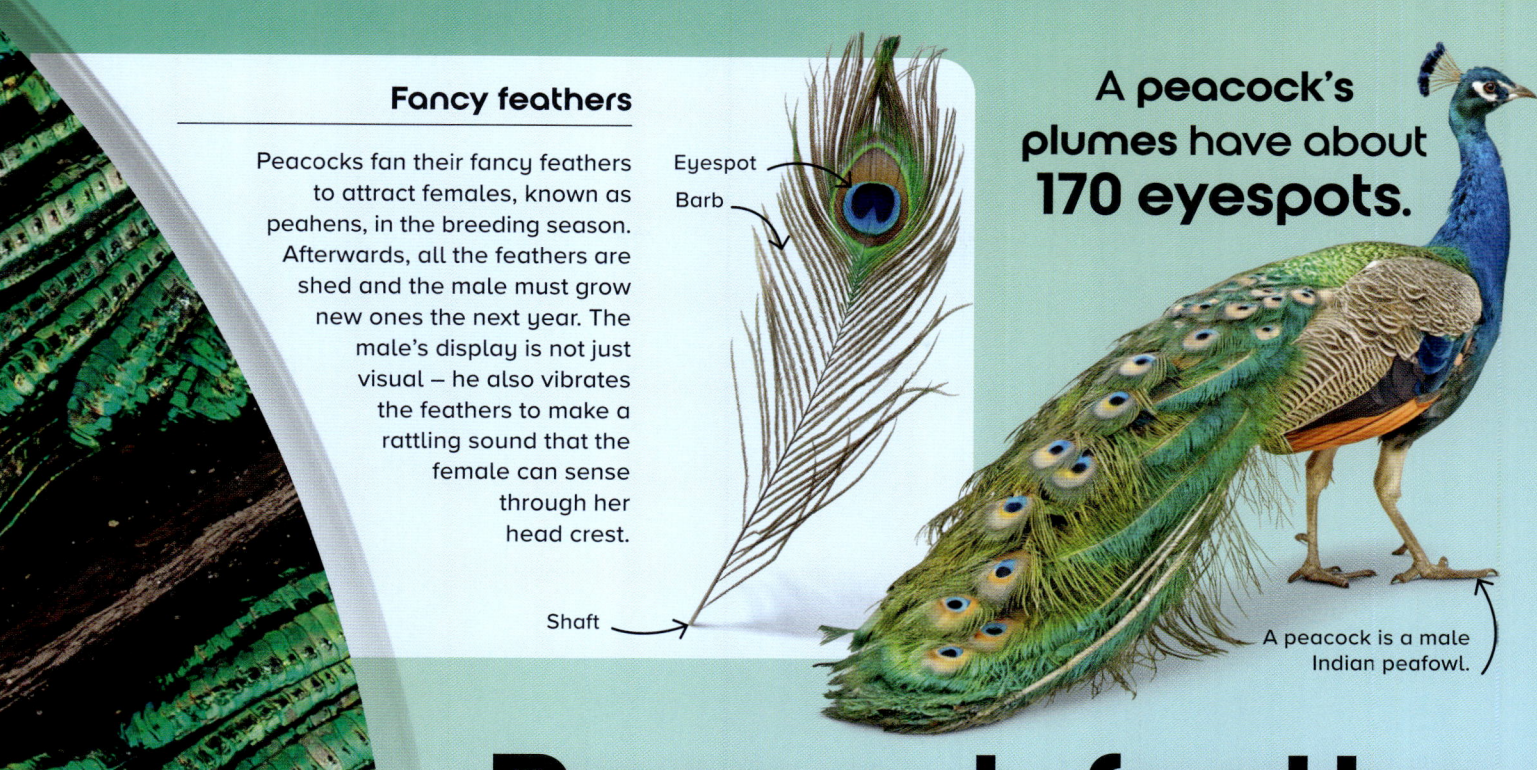

A peacock's plumes have about **170 eyespots**.

A peacock is a male Indian peafowl.

Eyespot
Barb
Shaft

Peacock feather

Peacocks and many other birds have feathers that are iridescent, which means their colours shimmer and change when they move, like the colours on a soap bubble. This beautiful effect is caused mostly by the physical structure of the feathers and not by chemical pigments.

How it works: Iridescence

Iridescence is also sometimes called structural colouration because the effect comes from microscopic structures in the feathers. These tiny structures contain many layers that reflect light from lots of different places. The reflected light rays interfere with one another, which strengthens certain colours. If the angle of the light changes, so does the interference pattern, which is why the colours shimmer as the bird moves.

Anna's hummingbird

The pink and green colours of this hummingbird come from iridescence.

Ultraviolet vision

Like most birds, peacocks can see more colours than humans can. As well as all the colours of the rainbow, a bird's eye can detect ultraviolet (UV) light. Feathers that look drab to us are often filled with colour and patterns when viewed in UV light. Scientists think that these extra markings help birds find mates.

Visible light
To human eyes, the barred owl has creamy white and brown feathers.

UV light
Birds see different colours, like the vivid patches on the underside of the wings.

Peacock feather | The natural world

Flight muscles

Insects beat their wings by squeezing sets of muscles in their thorax (the middle part of the body) in and out. Dragonflies are unique because these muscles are attached directly to the base of their wings. This allows them to control each wing independently. There are two sets of muscles: one that swings the wing up, the other moving it down.

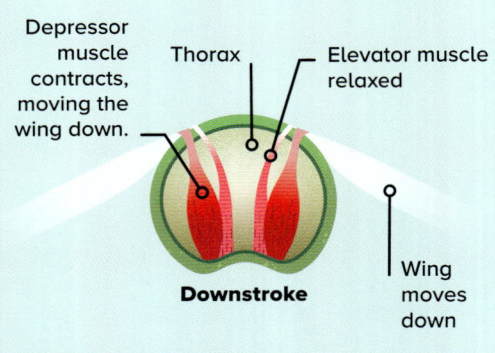

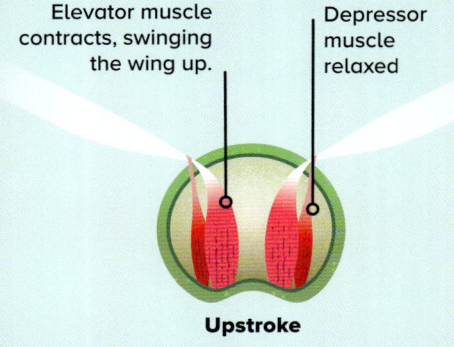

Waterproofing

A dragonfly's wings are remarkably waterproof, ensuring that water doesn't affect its ability to fly. Tiny spikes on the veins and a layer of wax on the membrane force water to form into droplets, preventing it from spreading out. There are also ridges and valleys on the wing, which help channel beads of water away.

How it works: Wing patterns

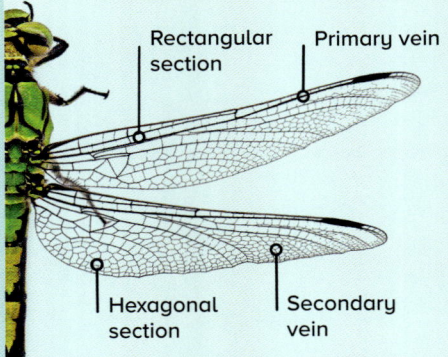

The wing structure is made up of long, straight primary veins and smaller secondary veins, which give each tiny section of the wing membrane its shape. Sections at the front edge of the wing are rectangular. These are stiff and strong, helping the dragonfly cut into the wind as it flies. Hexagonal sections at the back of the wing make it more flexible, allowing it to bend for greater control.

Dragonfly wing

Dragonflies are the fastest flyers of the insect world, able to reach speeds of 58 kph (36 mph). They are also amazingly agile: they can fly backwards, snap up prey mid-air with perfect accuracy, and even take off vertically like a helicopter. Looking at a dragonfly wing up close reveals some of the structures that enable such dazzling feats.

Dragonflies have two pairs of wings. Each wing is able to move independently.

Dragonflies are the most expert predators on Earth, with a hunting success rate of 97 per cent.

Huge compound eyes give all-round vision to spot prey in mid-air.

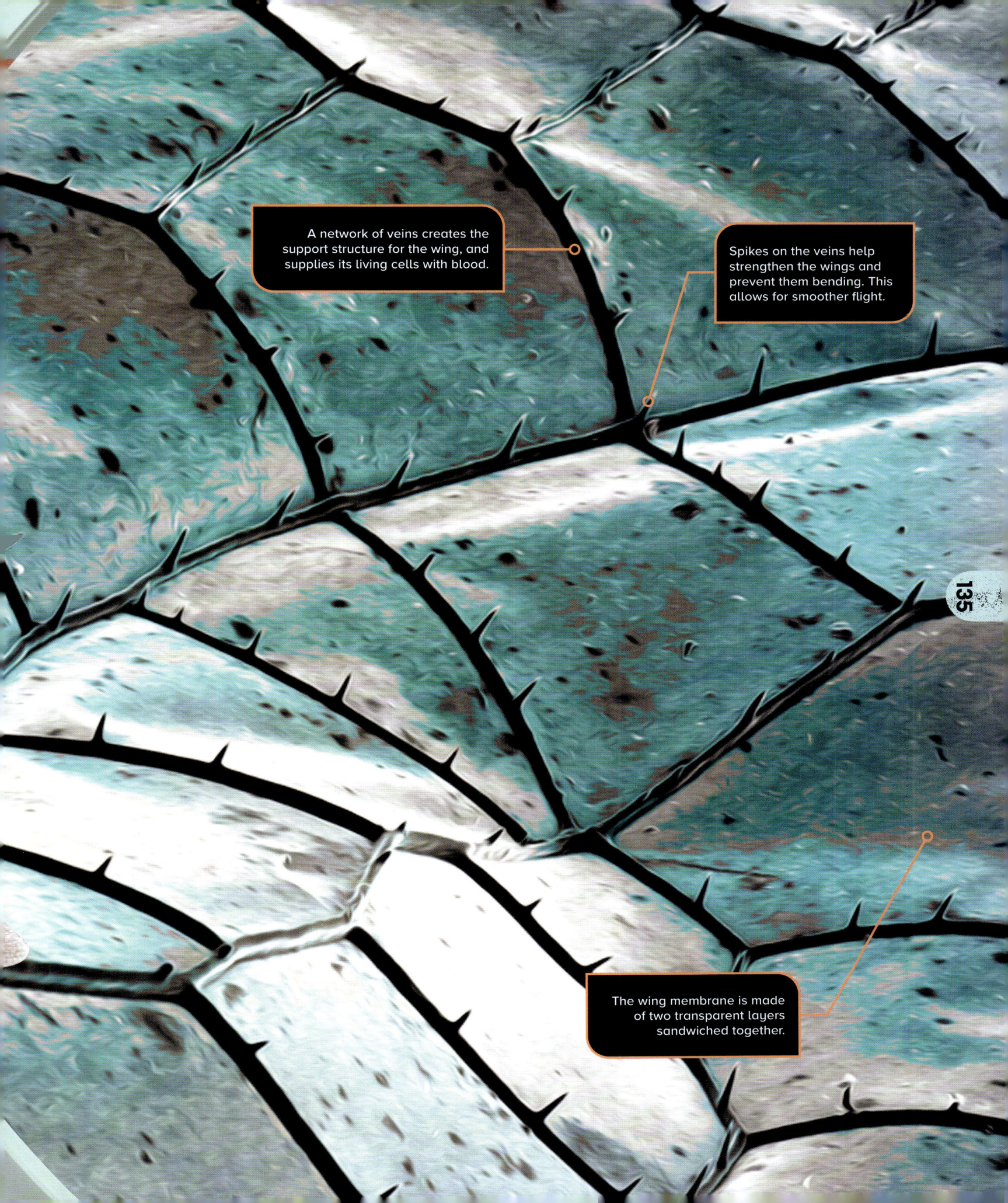

The bottom of a gecko's foot is covered in hundreds of thousands of tiny hairlike structures called setae. These setae can be a thousand times thinner than a human hair.

The ends of each seta branch into several hundred even finer structures called spatulae. These give each toe a large surface area to help it grip.

The toe pad flattens and spreads out when touching a solid surface.

Geckos stick to **almost all surfaces** except **Teflon**, which is used to coat non-stick pans.

How it works: Gecko feet

Geckos' feet rely on a very faint force of attraction that occurs when two objects touch. The billions of tiny fibres on their toes increase the area of contact between their feet and the surface, maximizing the force of attraction. The force is strong enough to stop the gecko from falling, even when it's upside down.

Tokay gecko

Spatulae are just ten millionths of a millimetre wide.

Gecko foot

Anyone who's seen a gecko run up a wall or across a ceiling might think the little lizards have sharp claws or glue-tipped toes. In fact, as this close-up image shows, they have special toe pads covered with what look like millions of tiny hairs. These give gecko feet their incredibly powerful grip.

Fly foot

Flies can walk on ceilings too, but they do it in a different way from geckos. Their feet have tiny claws to cling to rough surfaces. Each foot also has two pads called pulvilli that make a sticky fluid to grip smooth surfaces.

Pulvilli

Claw

Walking on walls

Spiders stick to walls just like geckos, using tiny hairs on their feet to create an attraction. Like geckos, they can release each foot, with a slight twist that changes the angle of contact with the wall, reducing the force of attraction.

Lesser house spider

Streamlined swimmers

A shark has a torpedo-shaped body ideal for swimming fast. Its powerful tail fin flicks from side to side, propelling the shark forwards, while two pectoral fins control steering. The dorsal fin keeps it stable. A flexible skeleton made from cartilage – a rubbery tissue lighter than bone – enables the shark to twist and turn at high speed.

Gills for breathing
Dorsal fin for stability
Cartilage backbone for flexible movement
Tail fin for forward propulsion
Oil-rich liver helps the shark to stay afloat
Pectoral fin for steering

Sharkskin

Sharks look smooth from a distance, but if you ever dared to stroke one, it would feel as rough as sandpaper. Their skin is covered in a layer of toothlike scales called denticles, each smaller than a full stop. Denticles help to guide water efficiently around sharks' bodies, letting them swim fast with hardly any effort.

Blacktip reef shark

18th-century violin makers used sharkskin as sandpaper.

Shark-inspired tech

Inspired by sharks and their speed in the water, scientists, engineers, and designers have studied their skin and tried to copy how it works. Speed-enhancing swimsuits and barnacle-busting paints are two inventions that imitate the shape and structure of a shark's denticles.

Speedy swimsuits
This fabric, which mimics the ridges of denticles, has been used to make high-performance swimsuits. The swimsuits let wearers glide through water with less resistance, just like a shark, but they are banned at the Olympics as they give an unfair advantage.

Sharkskin paint
Whales and boats get covered in small animals called barnacles, but sharks don't as their rough skin is hard for baby barnacles to stick to. Scientists have developed a special rough-textured paint that works the same way, keeping boats free of this nuisance.

Glossary

Adhesive A substance that sticks things together, such as glue.

Algae Simple, plantlike organisms that mostly live in water and make their food by photosynthesis.

Antenna A sensitive feeler on the head of an insect or other small animal.

Bacteria Microscopic, single-celled organisms that have no cell nuclei. Bacteria live in every kind of habitat and make up one of the main kingdoms of life.

Biodegradable Able to break down and decay naturally.

Bioluminescence Production of light by an organism. The light is generated by a chemical reaction.

Blood A fluid that circulates through the body of an animal delivering vital substances and removing waste chemicals.

Capillary action The flow of a liquid such as water into a narrow space due to attraction between the water molecules and the surrounding surface.

Carbon dioxide A gas released as a waste product by living things. Plants use carbon dioxide in photosynthesis.

Cell A tiny unit of living matter. Cells are the building blocks of all living things.

Cell wall Structural layer around the outside of the cell membrane in some kinds of organisms, such as bacteria, plants, fungi, and most algae.

Cellulose A substance found in plant cell walls that strengthens the cells and helps support the whole plant.

Chalk A soft, white rock formed from fossilized microorganisms that live in the sea.

Chemical reaction A process in which one or more substances (reactants) are transformed into new substances (products) by the breaking and formation of chemical bonds in molecules.

Chitin A tough, fibrous substance that makes up cell walls of fungi and the exoskeletons of insects and other small animals.

Chloroplast A tiny structure in a plant cell where photosynthesis takes place.

Cilia Tiny, moving hairlike structures on cells.

Clot A sticky lump that forms when blood thickens.

Composite material A material made from several different substances.

Compound eye An eye made up of many tiny light-detecting units, each with its own lens. Insects have compound eyes.

Condense Turn from a gas to a liquid.

Coral A small marine animal that catches food with stinging tentacles. Some corals live in large colonies protected by a hard skeleton.

Cornea The curved, transparent front part of the human eye.

Crystal A solid material with a regular shape resulting from the ordered arrangement of its atoms or molecules.

Cuticle A protective outer layer on part of an animal or plant.

Decomposition The natural breakdown of dead organic matter through the action of microorganisms and fungi that feed on it.

Electron A negatively charged particle that occupies the outer part of an atom.

Electron microscope A microscope that uses a beam of electrons instead of a beam of light to create images, allowing greater magnification than a light microscope.

Embryo A very early stage in the development of an animal or plant after a male sex cell fertilizes a female sex cell (egg).

Enamel The very hard substance that forms the outer part of teeth.

Enzyme A substance in living things that speeds up a chemical reaction.

Evaporate Change from liquid to gas. When water evaporates, it turns into invisible water vapour in the air.

Exoskeleton A hard outer skeleton, such as that of insects and spiders, which supports and protects the body.

Fabric A material made by weaving fibres together. Fabrics are used to make clothes, bedding, carpets, and furniture.

Fibres Thin threads.

Forensic scientist A scientist who collects evidence to help solve crimes.

Fossil fuel A fuel formed from fossilized remains of living things. Coal, petrol, and natural gas are fossil fuels.

Friction A dragging force that occurs when one object rubs against another.

Gills Organs used by fish and other aquatic animals to breathe underwater.

Hornet A large wasp.

Hyphae Very fine threads that grow from a fungus into the organic matter it feeds on.

Immune system A body's defences against microorganisms that cause disease.

Invertebrate An animal without a backbone, such as an insect or worm.

Ion An atom or group of atoms that has lost or gained electrons and therefore has a positive or negative charge.

Iridescent An iridescent object has bright, shiny colours that change when viewed from different angles.

Keratin The tough protein that forms fur, hair, feathers, nails, horns, and hooves.

Kinetic energy The energy stored in a moving object.

Larva The early stage in the life cycle of an animal that undergoes a major change when it develops into an adult. A caterpillar is a larva.

Limestone Sedimentary rock formed by compaction of sediments rich in calcium carbonate, such as the remains of microscopic sea life.

Metamorphosis A dramatic change in the body of an animal as it develops. Caterpillars turn into butterflies by metamorphosis.

Microorganism An organism too small to be seen with the naked eye, such as a bacterium.

Mould A powdery, speckled, or fuzzy growth that appears on decaying organic matter and is made by fungi.

Mucus A thick, slimy liquid produced by animals for protection or to make a surface moist and slippery.

Nectar A sugary liquid produced by flowers. Bees use nectar to make honey.

Nerve A bundle of specialized cells that carries electrical signals around an animal's body.

Nymph The young of an insect that differs from the adult mainly in having undeveloped wing buds.

Organ A specialized part of an animal or plant that carries out a particular task, such as a stomach or a brain.

Ovary An organ in a female animal or plant that produces egg cells (female sex cells).

Oxygen A gas that makes up 21 per cent of Earth's atmosphere. Most living things take in oxygen from the air and use it to release energy from food in a process called respiration.

Parasite An organism that lives on or inside another organism (a host) and feeds on it, causing harm.

Pathogen A small parasitic organism that causes disease. Most pathogens are microscopic.

Pheromone A chemical produced by an animal that affects another member of the same species. Many pheromones are scents.

Phloem A system of microscopic tubes that carry sugars and other food substances around a plant.

Photosynthesis The process by which plants use the Sun's energy to make food molecules from water and carbon dioxide.

Phytoplankton Algae (plantlike organisms) that float in water and make food by photosynthesis.

Pigment A substance that gives colour to a cell or other object.

Pitch How high or low a sound is. Sounds of higher pitch have a higher frequency.

Plankton Organisms that drift in water and cannot swim against the currents. Most are microscopic.

Plaque A substance containing bacteria that builds up on the surface of teeth if they aren't brushed regularly. Plaque causes tooth decay.

Plastic A synthetic substance produced by a chemical process that creates long, chainlike molecules. Plastics are usually lightweight, flexible, and very durable.

Pollen A powder that contains male sex cells and is produced by flowers.

Pollinator An animal such as a bee that transfers pollen from flower to flower, helping plants reproduce.

Polyester A plastic often used to make synthetic fabrics.

Proboscis An elongated nose or snout on an animal, usually used for feeding.

Protein A substance made by living things from a chain of simpler units called amino acids. Proteins are used for building body tissues and for controlling the complex chemistry inside cells.

Retina A layer of light-sensitive cells lining the inside of an eye.

Rust A flaky, crystalline substance that forms when iron reacts with oxygen to form iron oxide.

Saliva A digestive liquid produced in an animal's mouth.

Salt The mineral sodium chloride, also called table salt. The word salt is also used for other compounds formed when an acid reacts with a base.

Salt flats A flat expanse of land covered with salt, usually in a desert. Salt flats are the remains of ancient lakes that dried out.

Scanning electron microscope (SEM) A microscope that produces images of 3D objects by bouncing electrons off their surface.

Sedimentary rock A kind of rock formed by compression of sediment (such as mud or sand) over millions of years. Chalk and limestone are sedimentary rocks.

Silk A natural fibre produced by animals such as spiders (to make webs and egg cases) and moths (to make cocoons). The word silk can also refer to fabrics made from silk.

Sodium chloride The scientific name for table salt. Sodium chloride is the main mineral in seawater.

Solvent A substance (usually a liquid) that can dissolve another substance to make a solution. For example, water can dissolve salt to make a solution.

Sound wave A vibration (back-and-forth movement) that travels through air or water. The sense of hearing relies on detection of sound waves by ears.

Spores Tiny reproductive structures made by seedless plants, fungi, and many microorganisms. A spore can grow into a new organism.

Starch An edible substance that plants use to store energy in seeds, roots, and other structures. Starch molecules consist of chains of sugar molecules bonded together.

Steel Iron with a small amount of carbon mixed into it. Steel is stronger than iron, less brittle, and rusts more slowly.

Synthetic Created chemically by people, rather than naturally occurring.

Tardigrade Also called a water bear, a tiny, very tough animal that has eight legs and lives in damp habitats such as moss.

Tissue A group of similar cells that make up part of an organism, such as muscle in animals.

Trilobite A prehistoric sea animal that belongs to a group of jointed-legged animals called arthropods, which also includes insects and spiders.

Turbulence A chaotic, often swirling, pattern of movement in a liquid or gas.

Ultraviolet (UV) light A form of light that is invisible to human eyes but visible to many other animals, including bees and birds.

Vacuum An empty space that contains no air or gas.

Venom A harmful fluid that an animal injects into another animal with a stinger or teeth.

Vibration Rapid back-and-forth movement. Vibration of solid objects creates sound waves.

Virus A kind of germ that invades a living cell and gets the cell to make new copies of the virus.

Water vapour The invisible gas that liquid water turns into.

Weathering The gradual crumbling and wearing away of rock on Earth's surface due to exposure to rain, wind, ice, and the action of plants and animals.

Xylem A system of microscopic tubes that carry water and minerals from the roots of plants to leaves.

Yeast A single-celled fungus. Some kinds of yeast are used to make bread and alcoholic drinks.

Index

A
achenes 104, 105
acoustic guitars 48
acrylic 19
adhesives 23
algae 86, 90–91, 113
allergies 26
amphibians 82
animals 28–29, 62, 100
antennae 64, 123
antifreeze 82
ants 126
apocrine glands 62
astronauts 12, 14, 114
atoms 30

B
baby teeth 73
bacteria 33, 35, 36, 88–89
  human body 8, 62, 73, 76–77
bags, carrier 42–43
ballpoint pens 16–17
bananas 106–107
barbs 121, 126, 132
barnacles 138
bed bugs 28
bees 98, 102, 126
beetles 28, 29, 80
bicycle helmets 44
biodegradable bags 42
bioluminescence 90
birds 133
Bíró, László 17
blades, razor 46–47
blood 8, 58–59, 122
blood flukes 70
butterflies 97, 130–131
butternut squashes 104

C
Cai Lun 21
capillary action 18, 19
carbon 86
carpet beetles 28
carrier bags 42–43
cat fleas 29
caterpillars 38, 97
cats 29, 62
cellulose 20, 91
cement 52, 53
chalk 86–87
chemical reactions 50, 55
chlorophyll 107
chloroplasts 90, 91, 93
chromatography 18
cilia 64, 65, 112
clay 52
clones 107, 112
coccolithophores 86, 87
colour (pigment) 17, 18, 130
comb jellies 112
combustion 50
composite flowers 102
compound eyes 128–129, 134
concrete 52–53, 85
copepods 113
cotton 24, 38
crabs 113, 129
crystals 30–31, 82–83
cups, disposable 44–45
cuticles 69, 92, 93, 115
cyanobacteria 88
cytoplasm 90

D
daisies 102–103
decomposition 42
de Mestral, Georges 12
dendrochronology 110
denticles 120–121, 138–139
dentine 73
dermis 60, 69
digestive systems 76–77
dinoflagellates 113
diseases 41, 76, 122
dispersal, seed 100
dogs 62
dragonflies 129, 134–135
dust 24–25, 26–27
dust mites 8, 26–27

E
earthworms 118–119
eccrine glands 62
eggs 26, 70, 114, 117
electric guitars 48
elephants 21, 62
enamel 72, 73, 139
enzymes 109

epidermis 60, 61, 63
ethylene 107
extremophiles 88
eyelash mites 70
eyes 66–67, 128–129

F
fabric 38–39, 40–41, 138
face masks 40–41
feathers 132–133
feet, gecko 136–137
felt-tip pens 18–19
fibrin 58
fingernails 60
fingerprints 60
fins 138
fish 85, 112
fleas 29, 112
Fleming, Alexander 35
flies 28, 128–129, 137
florets 102, 103
flowers 98, 102–103, 104, 108
follicles 60, 62, 69, 70
forensic science 98
fossils 86
friction 50
frogs 82, 117
frost 82
fruit flies 28
fruits 33, 104, 107
fungal spores 24, 34–35

G
galvanized metals 55
gecko feet 136–137
germination 100
gills 116, 117
glands 62, 69, 124, 127
glass 50, 85
glues 23
goosebumps 69
guitar strings 48–49

H
haemoglobin 59
hair 24, 64, 68–69, 70–71
  gecko feet 136, 137
  plant 97, 108–109
  see also follicles
hazelnuts 104

hazmat suits 41
head lice 70–71
helmets, bicycle 44
heterochromia 66
hibernation 114
hibiscus 95, 99
histamine 122, 127
hooks (fasteners) 12, 14, 15
hornet stings 126–127
horseflies 128–129
hulls 101
hyphae 35
hypodermis 60

I
ice 30, 82–83
immune systems 122
infections 41, 89, 122
  see also viruses
influenza virus 8
ink 16–17, 18–19
iridescence 130, 133
irises 66–67
iron 54–55

K
kelp 90
keratin 60, 69
kingfishers 12
kitchen sponges 36–37

L
lacewings 124
larvae 26, 112, 113, 124
leaves 92–95
leeches 118
lice, head 70–71
light microscopy 6
limestone 52
linen 39
lobsters 129
lotus leaves 94

M
macrophotography 7
magnification 6
malaria 122
matchsticks 50–51
melanin 66, 69
membrane 134, 135

metals 46, 48, 54–55
micrometeorites 24
microplastics 24, 42
microscopes 6–7
microspheres 22, 23
mites 8, 26–27, 70, 114
molecules 18, 64, 80
mosquitoes 122–123
moss mites 114
moss piglets 114
moths 38, 64, 124
mould 34–35
mucus 64
muscles 66, 75, 134
mushrooms 35

N

nails 60
nectar 98, 102, 122
nematodes 114
nibs 17
nits 71
noses 64–65, 75
notes, sticky 22–23
nylon 13, 39, 48, 49
nymphs 26, 70

O

oleic acid 16
olives 95, 104
olivine 84
ommatidia 128, 129
oxidation 55

P

packing peanuts 44
paints 138
paper 17, 18, 20–21
   see also sticky notes
papillae 74–75
parasites 28, 70–71, 122
parrotfish 85
pathogens 58
peacocks 132–133
penicillin 35
pens 16–19
peppercorns 32–33
peppermint leaves 94
phloem cells 110
phosphorus 50

photosynthesis 86, 93
phytoplankton 113
pigment 17, 18, 130
pigs 62
pitch 48
plankton 112–113
plant fibres 20–21, 22
plaque 72, 73
plasma 58
plastic fibres 18, 39, 40, 42
platelets 58
pollen 8, 24, 65, 98–99
pollution 24, 42
polyamides 19
polyester 13, 19, 39
polystyrene foam 44–45
pond skaters 80
poo 21, 26, 76–77, 85
pores 62–63, 74, 92–93
prehistoric tools 23, 47
pressure 47
proboscis 122, 123
protective clothing 40–41
pulvilli 137
pupils 66–67

R

radulae 121
raindrops 80–81
razor blades 46–47
recycling 20, 35, 42, 44
red blood cells 58–59
reinforced concrete 52
retinas 66
rings, trees 110–111
Romans, ancient 52, 73
rotifers 114
rust 54–55

S

saliva 73, 75, 122
salt 9, 30–31
sand 24, 52, 84–85
sandstone 85
scales 130–131, 138–139
sea sponges 36, 84, 86
sebum 69
seeds 12, 100–101, 104, 107
SEM (Scanning Electron
   Microscopy) 7

sesame seeds 100–101
setae 136
shark skin 138–139
shaving foam 46
ships 55
shock absorbers 44, 73
shrimps 129
silica 97
silk 38, 64, 124–125
silkworms 38, 124
silverfish 29
skin 24, 60–61, 62–63, 89
   sharks 138–139
   see also follicles
smell 62, 64, 76
snails 120–121
snot 64–65
snowflakes 82–83
sodium chloride 30
soil 35, 98, 118
sound waves 48
spatulae 136, 137
spicules 84
spiders 124–125, 137
spigots 125
spinnerets 124
spirogyra 90–91
sponges, kitchen 36–37
spores
   fungal 24, 34–35
   pollen 8, 24, 65, 98–99
starch 42–43
steel 17, 46, 52, 55
sticky notes 22–23
stingers, hornet 126–127
stinging nettles 96–97
stomata 92, 93
strawberries 104–105
strings, guitar 48–49
sugars 25, 93
sunflowers 102
surface tension 80
sweat pores 62–63
swimsuits 138
synthetic fabrics 24, 39

T

tadpoles 116–117
tapeworms 70
tar 23

tardigrades 9, 114–115
taste buds 74, 75
teeth 72–73, 116, 121
Teflon 137
TEM (Transmission Electron
   Microscopy) 7
tomatoes 34–35, 95
tongues 74–75, 120–121
toothbrushes 72
toothpastes 73
trains 12
tree rings 110–111
trichomes 94–95
trigger hairs 108
trilobites 129
tungsten carbide 17

U, V

ultraviolet (UV) 18, 102, 133
vacuum cleaners 24
veins 130, 134, 135
Velcro 12–13
venom 97, 121, 127
Venus flytraps 108–109
viruses 8, 58, 76
   see also infections
volcanic rock 85

W

water 36, 55, 80–81, 90
water bears 114
waterproofing 134
webspinners 124
wedges 14
weevils 29
white blood cells 58
wind 98, 100
wings 130–131, 134–135
wool 38
World War II 17
worms 114, 118–119, 124

X, Y, Z

xylem cells 110, 111
zips 14–15
zooplankton 113

Acknowledgments

Dorling Kindersley would like to thank Nikon Small World for help sourcing images; Remi Yuter at Hot Paper Lantern for help sourcing images; Katie John for proofreading; Elizabeth Wise for the index; Steve Crozier for photo retouching; Aditya Katyal for picture research assistance; Samrajkumar S. for picture research admin support; and Rakesh Kumar, Rashika Kachroo, Dheeraj Arora, and Romi Chakraborty for help with jacket design.

The publisher would also like to thank the following for their kind permission to reproduce their photographs:

(Key: a-above; b-below/bottom; c-centre; f-far; l-left; r-right; t-top)

1 Science Photo Library: Alex Hyde. **2-3 Pierre Anquet**. **4 Alamy Stock Photo:** Science Photo Library / Steve Gschmeissner (tr). **4-5 Shutterstock.com:** Ireneusz Waledzik (bc). **5 Alamy Stock Photo:** Nerthuz (cl). **Martin Oeggerli:** © Martin Oeggerli (Micronaut) 2022, supported by H Halbritter and R Buchner, University Vienna (tr); © Martin Oeggerli (Micronaut) 2023, supported by L Howard, EM Facility, Dartmouth College. (cr). **6-139 Adobe Stock:** Koosen (Acrylic Block). **6-144 Shutterstock.com:** Miloje (Page Number Box). **6 Alamy Stock Photo:** Albazil (cr); Panther Media Global / Fyletto (crb); Blickwinkel / F. Fox (br). **Dreamstime.com:** Elena Schweitzer / Egal (bl). **Science Photo Library:** Omikron (c). **7 Alamy Stock Photo:** Inga Spence (bc); Javier Torrent / VWPics (tr). **Science Photo Library:** Steve Gschmeissner (tl); Northwestern University / Laurence Marks (bl). **8 Alamy Stock Photo:** Nerthuz (bc). **Science Photo Library:** Steve Gschmeissner (bc/Bacterium, clb, br); NAID / National Institutes Of Health (cl, bl). **8-9 Science Photo Library:** Steve Gschmeissner (bc). **9 Alamy Stock Photo:** Science Photo Library / Steve Gschmeissner (bl). **Nanofab:** Dr. Todd Simpson, Western Nanofabrication Facility, London, Canada (r). **10-11 Science Photo Library:** Eye Of Science (bc). **10 Macrofying / Ole Bielfeldt:** (t). **11 Science Photo Library:** Juergen Berger (tr); Eye Of Science (cla); Power And Syred (br). **12 Alamy Stock Photo:** FLPA (tl); Ulana Switucha (cr). **Getty Images / iStock:** Svetik15 (br). **NASA:** (clb). **Shutterstock.com:** Abubakar0023 (c). **12-13 Science Photo Library:** Juergen Berger. **14 Alamy Stock Photo:** Roland & Renate Kraft (bc). **14-15 Science Photo Library:** Power And Syred. **16 Macrofying / Ole Bielfeldt**. **17 Dreamstime.com:** Sergio Delle Vedove (crb); Иван Масюк (c). **Getty Images / iStock:** Liubov Khutter-Kukkonin (ca). **Shutterstock.com:** John Doyle Images (bc); Monbibi (cr). **18 Dreamstime.com:** Prillfoto (ca). **Science Photo Library:** Andrew Lambert Photography (clb). **18-19 Science Photo Library:** Power And Syred. **20 Shutterstock.com:** Loner Nguyen (cb). **20-21 Nanofab:** Dr. Todd Simpson, Western Nanofabrication Facility, London, Canada (b). **21 Alamy Stock Photo:** Heritage Image Partnership Ltd / Fine Art Images (tr). **Shutterstock.com:** Studio 11 (tc). **22-23 Science Photo Library:** Volker Steger. **23 Paul Kozowyk:** (bc). **Shutterstock.com:** Swavo (ca). **24-25 Science Photo Library:** Eye Of Science. **24 Alamy Stock Photo:** Andrew Paterson (tr). **Bridgeman Images:** © Look and Learn (cb). **Dr Sherri A Mason:** (cla/Microplastics). **Science Photo Library:** Dennis Kunkel Microscopy (cla); Steve Gschmeissner (tl, tc, c/ Microplastic Bobble); Kateryna Kon (c); Science Source / Ted Kinsman (bl). **Shutterstock.com:** Remini Marum (cl). **26 Science Photo Library:** Dennis Kunkel Microscopy (bl, cb). **26-27 Science Photo Library:** Eye Of Science. **28 Adobe Stock:** Macroscopic Solution (tr). **Science Photo Library:** Eye Of Science (tl). **Shutterstock.com:** Tomasz Klejdysz (tl/x4); Ireneusz Waledzik (bl). **29 Alamy Stock Photo:** Pawich Sattalerd (cr); Stefan Sollfors (br). **Science Photo Library:** Eye Of Science (tr); Steve Gschmeissner (crb). **Shutterstock.com:** Tomasz Klejdysz (clb/x3); Tran The Ngoc (tc); Charly Morlock (cl). **30 Alamy Stock Photo:** Wild Places Photography / Chris Howes (cla). **Dreamstime.com:** Sara Winter (ca). **Science Photo Library:** Dirk Wiersma (bl). **30-31 Nanofab:** Dr. Todd Simpson, Western Nanofabrication Facility, London, Canada. **32-33 Science Photo Library:** Power And Syred. **33 Dreamstime.com:** Pakorn Kumruen (br); Shamils (tc). **Getty Images:** Universal Images Group / Universal History Archive (crb). **Shutterstock.com:** Valentyn Volkov (cb). **34-35 Science Photo Library:** Alex Hyde. **35 Dreamstime.com:** Bjorn Hovdal (br). **Science Photo Library:** Wim Van Egmond (bc); Alex Hyde (cla); Michael P. Gadomsk (cr). **36 Alamy Stock Photo:** Wolfgang Pölzer (bl); Wildlife GmbH (bc). **Dreamstime.com:** Italianestro (tc). **Science Photo Library:** Dennis Kunkel Microscopy (cl). **36-37 Science Photo Library:** Power And Syred. **38 Getty Images:** Connect Images / Albert Lleal Moya (cl). **Science Photo Library:** Steve Gschmeissner (tl); Susumu Nishinaga (cr). **39 Alamy Stock Photo:** Science Photo Library / Steve Gschmeissner (tr). **Science Photo Library:** Dr Jeremy Burgess (tl); Eye Of Science (br). **40-41 Science Photo Library:** Eye Of Science. **41 Getty Images / iStock:** E+ / FG Trade (bl). **Shutterstock.com:** Martin Lisner (br). **42-43 Science Photo Library:** Steve Gschmeissner. **42 Alamy Stock Photo:** Cavan Images / Christophe Launay (cl). **Shutterstock.com:** Chayanuphol (bc); Nito (crb). **44 Dreamstime.com:** Chernetskaya (br); Xxlphoto (cla). **Getty Images / iStock:** RG-vc (clb). **44-45 Science Photo Library:** Stefan Diller. **46-47 Science Photo Library:** Steve Gschmeissner. **47 Dorling Kindersley:** Natural History Museum / Harry Taylor (bc). **Dreamstime.com:** Andrei Kuzmik (bl); Martinmark (cr). **Science Photo Library:** Biophoto Associates (br). **48-49 Science Photo Library:** Power And Syred. **48 Dreamstime.com:** Nexus7 (bc); Spolcycstudio (cla). **Shutterstock.com:** Lahmz (clb). **50 Bridgeman Images:** Look and Learn / Bernard Platman Antiquarian Collection (tl). **Dreamstime.com:** Alexandr Kornienko (ca); Marazem (br). **Science Photo Library:** Charles D. Winters (bc). **Shutterstock.com:** Yuphayao Pooh's (cb). **51 Macrofying / Ole Bielfeldt**. **52-53 Science Photo Library:** Patrick Landmann / Lerm. **52 Alamy Stock Photo:** Imaginechina Limited (c); Mickey Lee (bl); Neighbors Cat - PW (br). **54-55 Science Photo Library:** Eye Of Science. **55 Dreamstime.com:** Domnitsky (c); Wirestock (cra). **Shutterstock.com:** Dina van Wyk (br). **56-57 Science Photo Library:** Dennis Kunkel Microscopy (bc). **56 Martin Oeggerli:** © M Oeggerli (Micronaut) 2015, supported by HP Marti, Swiss TPH, University Hospital Basel (bl). **Science Photo Library:** Lennart Nilsson, TT (tl); Martin Oeggerli (ca). **57 Martin Oeggerli:** © Martin Oeggerli (Micronaut) 2021, supported by University Hospital Basel (Pathology), and School (tl). **58-59 Science Photo Library:** Dennis Kunkel Microscopy. **58 Science Photo Library:** Eye Of Science (clb); Power And Syred (cr). **60-61 Science Photo Library:** Power And Syred. **60 Dreamstime.com:** GCapture (crb). **Science Photo Library:** Steve Gschmeissner (cl). **Shutterstock.com:** Wirestock Creators (c). **62-63 Science Photo Library:** POWER AND SYRED. **62 Alamy Stock Photo:** Sash Alexander (bc); Janne Turkka (crb). **Dreamstime.com:** Nils Jacobi (cb). **Getty Images / iStock:** selvanegra (bl). **64-65 Science Photo Library:** Dennis Kunkel Microscopy. **64 Science Photo Library:** BSIP VEM (cl); Ozgur Kerem Bulur (c). **66 Shutterstock.com:** Kotoimages (cb). **66-67 Suren Manvelyan**. **68-69 Science Photo Library:** Steve Gschmeissner. **69 Shutterstock.com:** Flystock (br). **70-71 Science Photo Library:** Martin Oeggerli. **70 Alamy Stock Photo:** Scenics & Science (tl); SuperStock / RGB Ventures / Centers of Disease Control (tc/x2). **Science Photo Library:** Steve Gschmeissner (clb, bc/Tapeworm); Natural History Museum, London (bc); Sinclair Stammers (br). **72-73 Science Photo Library:** Lennart Nilsson, TT. **73 Science Photo Library:** Dennis Kunkel Microscopy (bl). **Shutterstock.com:** Kalmati 123 (crb); Giuliano Del Moretto (bc). **74-75 Martin Oeggerli:** © Martin Oeggerli (Micronaut) 2021, supported by University Hospital Basel (Pathology), and School. **75 Dreamstime.com:** Chernetskaya (crb); Oleksii Terpugov (cb); Ruslan Gilmanshin (bc); Anastasiia Skorobogatova (br). **Shutterstock.com:** Grey_And (cr); Photoongraphy (c); New Africa (tr). **76 Martin Oeggerli:** © Martin Oeggerli (Micronaut) 2014, supported by Kenneth N. Goldie, Biozentrum Center for (bl). **Science Photo Library:** Steve Gschmeissner (cla). **76-77 Martin Oeggerli:** © M Oeggerli (Micronaut) 2015, supported by HP Marti, Swiss TPH, University Hospital Basel. **78-79 Alamy Stock Photo:** Javier Torrent / VWPics (tc). **78 Science Photo Library:** Steve Gschmeissner (br). **79 Sébastien Malo:** (tr). **Science Photo Library:** Dennis Kunkel Microscopy (cl); Steve Gschmeissner (br). **80 Alamy Stock Photo:** Blickwinkel / Lenke (bc); F1online Digitale Bildagentur GmbH / Matthias Lenke (br). **Getty Images:** Moment / TorriPhoto (bl). **80-81 naturepl.com:** Paul Bertner. **82 Alamy Stock Photo:** NorthScape (clb); Kay Roxby (cb); Paul Weston (bl); www.theuntravelledworld.com (bc); Christopher Price (br). **82-83 Science Photo Library:** Kenneth Libbrecht. **84-85 Zhang Chao**. **85 Alamy Stock Photo:** Nature Picture Library / Linda Pitkin (cra); Ronnybas (br). **Dreamstime.com:** Photka (c); Vadim Zh (bc). **Getty Images / iStock:** Uwe Moser (crb). **86 Alamy Stock Photo:** Stocker123 (cla). **Science Photo Library:** Natural History Museum, London (cb). **86-87 Science Photo Library:** Steve Gschmeissner. **88 Alamy Stock Photo:** Peter Adams Photography (cl). **88-89 Science Photo Library:** Steve Gschmeissner. **90 Alamy Stock Photo:** Antonio Busiello (bc). **Dreamstime.com:** Ioannaalexa (clb). **Getty Images / iStock:** RugliG (cla). **Shutterstock.com:** MuhsinRina (br). **90-91 Science Photo Library:** Marek Mis. **92-93 naturepl.com:** Alex Hyde. **93 Shutterstock.com:** Garmoncheg (bl). **94 Getty Images / iStock:** Kolesnikovserg (tl). **Martin Oeggerli:** © Martin Oeggerli (Micronaut) 2015, kindly supported by university Hospital Basel (Pathology) and (cl). **Science Photo Library:** Eye Of Science (br). **Shutterstock.com:** Shadow of the sun (cra). **95 123RF.com:** Plateresca (tc). **Alamy Stock Photo:** Science Photo Library (cl). **Dreamstime.com:** Fotofermer (crb). **Science Photo Library:** Eye Of Science (br); Martin Oeggerli (tr). **Shutterstock.com:** Grey_And (bc). **96-97 Science Photo Library:** Eye Of Science. **97 Alamy Stock Photo:** Imagebroker.com / Sunbird Images (br); Nature Picture Library / Kim Taylor (bc/Butterfly Egg). **Dreamstime.com:** Mikhail Kokhanchikov (bl); Sandra Standbridge (bc). **98 Alamy Stock Photo:** Tim Gainey (cl). **naturepl.com:** Phil Savoie (tl). **Shutterstock.com:** Just_ Flowerin (bc). **99 Martin Oeggerli:** © Martin Oeggerli (Micronaut) 2005. (tl); © Martin Oeggerli (Micronaut) 2022, supported by H Halbritter and R Buchner, University Vienna (tr); © Martin Oeggerli (Micronaut) 2023, supported by L Howard, EM Facility, Dartmouth College. (b). **100 Alamy Stock Photo:** Blickwinkel / Hecker (cb); Nature Picture Library / Jurgen Freund (bl); Nature Picture Library / Adrian Davies (bc); Imagebroker.com / Tuns (br). **Dreamstime.com:** Oleg Troino (clb). **Science Photo Library:** Power And Syred (cra). **100-101 Science Photo Library:** Power And Syred. **102 Dreamstime.com:** Vilor (br). **Science Photo Library:** Leonard Lessin (bl, bc). **102-103 Dr Haydn Bartlett**. **104 123RF.com:** Photomaru (tr); Utima (cr). **104-105 Science Photo Library:** Edward Kinsman. **106-107 Science Photo Library:** Dennis Kunkel Microscopy. **107 Dreamstime.com:** Lukasz Janyst (br). **Shutterstock.com:** New Africa (clb). **108 Alamy Stock Photo:** Custom Life Science Images (bl). **108-109 Science Photo Library:** Mona Lisa Production / Thierry Berrod. **110 Alamy Stock Photo:** Kevin Schafer (bl). **Shutterstock.com:** Triff (cr). **110-111 Science Photo Library:** Power And Syred. **112-113 Dreamstime.com:** Rsooll (Background). **112 Science Photo Library:** Marek Mis (bc); Alexander Semenov (tl); Nature Picture Library / Alex Mustard (tr). **113 Science Photo Library:** Dennis Kunkel Microscopy (clb); Shoma81 (tr); Steve Gschmeissner (crb). **114 Alamy Stock Photo:** Nature in Stock / Jan van Arkel (crb); Science Photo Library / Steve Gschmeissner (cla). **Dorling Kindersley:** ESO: NASA's Scientific Visualization Studio (cl). **Dreamstime.com:** Natika (bl). **Science Photo Library:** Eye Of Science (ca, cr, cb); Steve Gschmeissner (crb/Nematodes). **114-115 Science Photo Library:** Eye Of Science. **116-117 Getty Images:** Corbis Documentary / Clouds Hill Imaging Ltd.. **117 Alamy Stock Photo:** Blueshiftstudios / David Cook (tc); Nature Picture Library / MYN / Tim Hunt (cla, ca, cra); Dorling Kindersley ltd (crb); Anton Sorokin (bl). **naturepl.com:** Stephen Dalton (tr). **118 Alamy Stock Photo:** Graham Turner (cla). **Dreamstime.com:** Spectorfiona (clb). **Science Photo Library:** Louise Murray (cb). **118-119 Science Photo Library:** Steve Gschmeissner. **120-121 Alamy Stock Photo:** Papilio / Robert Pickett (tc). **Science Photo Library:** Eye Of Science. **121 Alamy Stock Photo:** Joe Belanger (bl); Jason Smalley Photography / AJS (br). **Dreamstime.com:** Roland Magnusson (tr). **Science Photo Library:** Volker Steger (bc). **122-123 Science Photo Library:** CDC. **122 Alamy Stock Photo:** Marek Slusarczyk (cb). **Getty Images / iStock:** E+ / Kerrick (bc). **124-125 Science Photo Library:** Dennis Kunkel Microscopy. **124 Alamy Stock Photo:** Li Ding (bc); Moehligdesign (bl); Life on white (br); Scenics & Science (cb). **Getty Images / iStock:** Mtreasure (c). **Science Photo Library:** George Bernard (cb/ Webspinners). **126 Science Photo Library:** Edward Kinsman (bl); Nicolas Reusens (br). **Shutterstock.com:** Irin-K (bc); MDong_97 (br/Fire ant). **126-127 Pierre Anquet**. **127 Alamy Stock Photo:** Nature Picture Library / Cyril Ruoso (c). **128-129 naturepl.com:** Thomas Marent. **129 Alamy Stock Photo:** Chris Mattison (cb); Stocktrek Images, Inc. / Bruce Shafer (bc). **Shutterstock.com:** Cornel Constantin (crb); Global Lighting (br). **130 naturepl.com:** Oliver Wright (tl). **Shutterstock.com:** New Africa (cr); Sebastian_Photography (c). **130-131 Sébastien Malo**. **132-133 Alamy Stock Photo:** Javier Torrent / VWPics. **133 Alamy Stock Photo:** Arsen Volkov (bl). **Dreamstime.com:** Evgeniya Moroz (tc). **Science Photo Library:** Science Source Inc. / Ted-Kinsman (bc, br). **Shutterstock.com:** Fatimadesigner (tr). **134 Getty Images / iStock:** Andreas Häuslbetz (tc); Mafrmcfa (bl). **naturepl.com:** Etienne Littlefair (br). **134-135 Alamy Stock Photo:** Connect Images / Sheri Neva. **136-137 Science Photo Library:** Power And Syred. **137 Alamy Stock Photo:** Dorling Kindersley ltd (tr); Viktoriia Ruban (bc); Minden Pictures / Stephen Dalton (br). **Dreamstime.com:** Isselee (bl). **Science Photo Library:** Power And Syred (tc). **138-139 Science Photo Library:** Ted Kinsman. **138 Alamy Stock Photo:** Imagebroker.com / Norbert Probst (c). **Getty Images:** Moment / Eko Prasetyo (bc). **139 Science Photo Library:** Eye Of Science (cb)

Cover images: Front: **Alamy Stock Photo:** Nerthuz cr; **Science Photo Library:** Dennis Kunkel Microscopy cra, Steve Gschmeissner tc, Kenneth Libbrecht br, Marek Mis bc, Power And Syred bl; **Zhang Chao:** cl; Back: **Alamy Stock Photo:** Nerthuz cl; **Science Photo Library:** Dennis Kunkel Microscopy cla, Steve Gschmeissner tc, Kenneth Libbrecht bl, Marek Mis bc, Power And Syred br; **Zhang Chao:** cr

DK Penguin Random House

Senior editors Amanda Wyatt, Ben Morgan
Senior art editor Emma Clayton
Managing editor Rachel Fox
Managing art editor Owen Peyton Jones
Production editor Gillian Reid
Production controller Ena Matagic
Jacket design Emma Clayton, Phil Ormerod
Editors Edward Aves, Ben Ffrancon Dowds, Jolyon Goddard
Designers Amy Child, Laura Gardner, Tory Gordon-Harris, Rhys Thomas
Illustration Diarmuid Ó Catháin
Picture research Deepak Negi
DTP designer Neeraj Bhatia
Publisher Andrew Macintyre
Art director Mabel Chan

Authors Clive Gifford, Tom Jackson, Nicola Temple
Consultants Derek Harvey, Penny Johnson

First published in Great Britain in 2026 by Dorling Kindersley Limited
20 Vauxhall Bridge Road,
London SW1V 2SA

The authorised representative in the EEA is Dorling Kindersley Verlag GmbH. Arnulfstr. 124, 80636 Munich, Germany

Copyright © 2026 Dorling Kindersley Limited
A Penguin Random House Company
10 9 8 7 6 5 4 3 2 1
001–352659–May/2026

All rights reserved.

No part of this publication may be reproduced, stored in or introduced into a retrieval system, or transmitted, in any form, or by any means (electronic, mechanical, photocopying, recording, or otherwise), without the prior written permission of the copyright owner.

No part of this publication may be used or reproduced in any manner for the purpose of training artificial intelligence technologies or systems. In accordance with Article 4[3] of the DSM Directive 2019/790, DK expressly reserves this work from the text and data mining exception.

A CIP catalogue record for this book is available from the British Library.
ISBN: 978-0-2417-7219-5

Printed and bound in China

www.dk.com

MIX
Paper | Supporting responsible forestry
FSC™ C018179
www.fsc.org

This book was made with Forest Stewardship Council™ certified paper – one small step in DK's commitment to a sustainable future.
Learn more at www.dk.com/uk/information/sustainability